'This book is much more than an account of a naive undertaking in the life of a rather strange man. For one thing, it radiates an intense intelligence and a candour that is never less than touching and, sometimes, downright heartrending. To have written so elegantly and often humorously about his mental health means Evans must now, to a great extent, be "better". But it's still an exercise in agonized soul-searching'   *Daily Mail*

'The real story of the book is about delusion and depression . . . Structurally, the book is smart: instead of beginning at the beginning, full of optimism and hope, it begins with Evans in a psychiatric unit, having been broken by the stresses of running his post-apocalyptic project . . . One imagines this must have been an incredibly painful book to write: the experiment happened nine years ago, and it's obviously taken this long for Evans to process and understand it'   *Guardian*

'Written in a prose style that could be described as "accessible scientific", *The Utopia Experiment* should probably be a mandatory handbook for any slightly nesh person fantasizing about living off-grid'   *Observer*

'[A] vivid, blackly comic account . . . Its message, I suspect, is that how we think about the world is often more a reflection of our own inner turmoil than an objective response to the very real problems around us . . . This is a thought-provoking tale, full of splendidly unlikely characters'   *Mail on Sunday*

'A gripping adventure story, even when (or especially when) things turn dark'   *Literary Review*

'The account of the collapse of the experiment is searingly honest; there is not a hint of self pity or recrimination against anyone but himself. The book makes fascinating reading'
                    Sydney Morning Herald

'An eccentric swirl of philosophy, comedy and wonderfully mad ideas. I loved it' Sam Mill   *. . . . . . . of Will Self*

D1322160

'For a memoir about the apocalypse and mental illness, *The Utopia Experiment* is unexpectedly upbeat. Evans' chatty narrative is laced with musings on technology, psychology and sociology, making for a thought-provoking read. It will leave you feeling that civilization, for all its discontents, maybe isn't quite so bad after all'
Big Issue

'A fun read – and a scary one'
BBC Focus

'In this perceptive and self-critical memoir, which took him some seven years to write, Evans asks why utopias so often turn into dystopias and why, despite that, people so often invest their hopes in them'
Saturday Paper (Australia)

'Excruciatingly honest and stranger than fiction . . . a riveting look at the eccentric world of doomers and preppers'
New Zealand Herald

'Evans always maintains a wry humour even as numerous uncertainties build into a breakdown. Never less than an engaging read, this book is a reminder of why the best utopias are those of our imaginations'
Sydney Morning Herald

'His observations are just wonderful. As well as being interesting and informative, he manages to inject humour into his writing'
Press & Journal

'A brave and insightful memoir'
Otago Daily Times

'A funny, gripping and unique real-life fable of hope, human nature and imminent apocalypse'
Will Storr,
author of *The Heretics*

'Here is a ponderment: Are you surprised at the high number of people who are crazy or the low number of people who are crazy? *The Utopia Experiment*, if the ponderment engages you, will help in your calculations'
Padgett Powell,
author of *The Interrogative Mood*

THE UTOPIA EXPERIMENT

Dylan Evans is an academic, philosopher and journalist. He has written several popular science books and was once described in *The Times* as 'the sort of polymath who makes you wonder what you've been doing with your brain'. He was born in Bristol and now lives in Guatemala.

Also by Dylan Evans

Atheism: All That Matters

Risk Intelligence: How to Live with Uncertainty

Placebo: Mind over Matter in Modern Medicine

Emotion: The Science of Sentiment

Introducing Evolutionary Psychology

Introducing Evolution

An Introductory Dictionary of Lacanian Psychoanalysis

DYLAN EVANS

THE UTOPIA EXPERIMENT

PICADOR

First published 2015 by Picador

This edition published 2015 by Picador
an imprint of Pan Macmillan
20 New Wharf Road, London N1 9RR
Associated companies throughout the world
www.panmacmillan.com

ISBN 978-1-4472-6130-8

1 3 5 7 9 8 6 4 2

A CIP catalogue record for this book is available from the British Library.

Printed and bound by CPI Group (UK) Ltd, Croydon, CR0 4YY

Visit **www.picador.com** to read more about all our books
and to buy them. You will also find features, author interviews and
news of any author events, and you can sign up for e-newsletters
so that you're always first to hear about our new releases.

This book is dedicated to

mental health nurses everywhere

– the unsung heroes of psychiatry

Have you ever thought that that ghastly catastrophe of fifty years ago was, well, was lucky for us? I know it sounds blasphemous; but mightn't it be that we've led more interesting lives than the perhaps rather pointless existence we would otherwise have been brought up to accept as life? We can see now that the values of the twentieth century were invalid; otherwise they wouldn't have wrecked the world. Don't you think the Accident has made us more appreciative of the vital things, like life itself, and like each other?

Brian Aldiss
Greybeard (1964)

There is, I am sensible, an age at which every one of you would choose to stop; and you will look out for the age at which, had you your wish, your species had stopped. Uneasy at your present condition for reasons which threaten your unhappy posterity with still greater uneasiness, you will perhaps wish it were in your power to go back; and this sentiment ought to be considered as the panegyric of your first parents, the condemnation of your contemporaries, and a source of terror to all those who may have the misfortune of succeeding you.

Jean-Jacques Rousseau
Discourse on the Origin and Basis of Inequality Among Men (1755)

Contents

1. THE SCREAM

An ear-splitting scream jolted me awake. I looked at the clock. It was 3 am.

The same voice cried out again in terror.

'No, please don't, NOOOO!'

I peered out of the window. Opposite was the locked ward. Was that where the scream came from? What on earth were they doing to the poor guy? I imagined a couple of brutal psychiatric nurses holding down a struggling patient while a doctor stabbed him with a gruesome syringe. I shook with fear.

It was my first night in the hospital. I had been detained under the Mental Health Act that afternoon for my own safety. I had never been a patient in a psychiatric hospital before, and I didn't know what to expect.

The place had appeared pleasant enough the previous afternoon. It was very modern, and I had my own room, with an en-suite bathroom and shower. But what about that scream? Suddenly those antiseptic corridors seemed very cold and sinister.

My fears had been sparked by a conversation with

another patient shortly after I had been admitted. As I paced around the enclosed patio, smoking furiously, a burly man in his twenties joined me in my circular walk. His biceps were tattooed and the knuckles on his right hand were bleeding. I didn't ask why. He stared at me for a while.

'Who's your doctor?' he asked suddenly.

'Dr Satoshi,' I replied.

'Oh no!' He grimaced, and shook his head. 'You poor bugger.'

At breakfast, I got my first sight of all the other patients on my ward. Well, all but one; apparently there was also a young woman called Rowena, but she almost always ate alone in her room.

I looked around the dining area. Three men in their forties and fifties, two women of similar ages, a young man in his late teens, and the burly patient I had met the day before. We sat around three small tables silently munching on breakfast cereal and thin slices of toast, until one of my companions greeted me in a refreshingly normal tone of voice.

'Good morning, I'm Terry. What's your name?'

'Hi. I'm Dylan,' I said. Unthinkingly, I reached out to shake his hand, but immediately wondered if this was rather too formal. What is the etiquette when introducing yourself to a fellow patient in a psychiatric hospital? It was not a question I had ever pondered before.

I struggled to think of an appropriate way of continuing. If we had been in prison, I could perhaps have asked what he was in for. Surely, I thought, the equivalent would be to ask someone what their diagnosis was, but that didn't seem quite right. Luckily, Terry relieved me of my dilemma by telling me he was here because his horrible wife had lied about him.

'That bloody woman!' he hissed. 'She's done this to me before, you know. Got me locked up when it suited her. I'm sure I'll get out soon, when the doctors realize she's the crazy one, not me!'

He sounded sane to me. For all I knew, he was telling the truth, and he was in fact the victim of some evil plot by his wife to get him out of the way. But as he told his tale, tiny cracks in the logic began to appear, and by the end I could see that his version of events might be somewhat skewed. Or might not. I really couldn't tell whether he was crazy. If I had met him in some other context, the question would not even have occurred to me.

Did his wife really call the police, for example, just to get Terry out of the way so she could enjoy the hotel on her own, as he maintained? Or was there something about his behaviour that prompted her call, which Terry was not telling me? Was she, perhaps, simply a concerned and loving wife trying to do the best for her deranged husband? Both scenarios seemed plausible. And neither seemed particularly bizarre.

My story was different. As I listened to Terry tell how

he had ended up here, in hospital, I cast around in my mind for a way to do the same. But every explanation I could think of made me sound like a complete nutcase. At least I was well enough to know how crazy I would sound if I told him the truth. So I kept my mouth shut, and just listened.

It's hard to seem normal in a mental hospital. Even the most innocent actions can seem suspicious when they are carried out by someone already labelled as crazy, as David Rosenhan noted in his famous 1973 paper, 'On being sane in insane places'. Rosenhan sent five healthy volunteers to several psychiatric hospitals in the United States and asked them to pretend to be mad. All were admitted and diagnosed with psychiatric disorders. After admission, the fake patients acted normally and told staff that they felt fine, and had not experienced any more hallucinations. Yet they were detained for an average of almost three weeks before being released. The nursing staff saw all their behaviour through the lens of mental illness. For example, when one volunteer was spotted making notes, nurses described him as engaging in 'writing behaviour', which they regarded with deep suspicion.

Dr Satoshi greeted me with a warm smile as I was ushered into his office. He gestured for me to sit down in the chair opposite him.

'How are you feeling today?'

'I'm OK,' I whispered. I kept touching my chin com-

pulsively, gripping individual hairs between the finger-
nails of my thumb and middle finger and tweaking them
out one by one. It's something I have done ever since,
whenever I feel nervous, and my friends tell me it looks
freakish and jittery, but at the time it felt strangely re-
assuring, a tiny area of my life where I retained a degree
of control.

'Do you think I'm bipolar?' I asked.

'I don't think so, but I can't say for sure yet,' he
replied.

I breathed a sigh of relief.

'I really don't want to go on one of those strong drugs
they give to people with bipolar disorder,' I pleaded.
'Several friends of mine are bipolar and I've seen a
couple of them when they were dosed up. It looks awful.'

'Dr Williams thought you might be suffering from
bipolar disorder when we admitted you yesterday. Do
you know why she thought that?'

'Yes.'

I looked down at the floor. I had been thinking
the same thing. Many of the signs seemed to fit. I was
obviously depressed, but during the preceding months
my behaviour might well have been described as manic.

'Why don't you think I'm bipolar?'

'It was too systematic. You spent months planning
your experiment. A lot of organization went into it. A
typical manic phase wouldn't last that long, or allow
such careful thought.'

'So you believe me, then? The stuff about my experiment? You know it's not just all a delusion?'

'Yes, Dylan. We did some Googling, and we found some newspaper articles about your experiment. I can't blame Dr Williams for thinking your tale was delusional. I mean all that stuff about your followers, and preparing for the end of the world! But it seems it's all true.'

It wasn't quite true, but the gist was correct. We didn't *really* think the world was about to end. Or at least, we didn't *start off* thinking that way. The whole experiment was, in fact, meant to be a simulation. We would try to figure out what life might be like *if* civilization collapsed, by acting as if it already had. It was to be a kind of collaborative storytelling, a real-life role-play.

It was a very vague plan, but the basic idea had felt compelling at the time. Now, two years later, it seemed absurd. Why had it become an overriding obsession, leading me to sell my house and give up my academic career to pursue it? How had everything come crashing down around me, ending in my flight from the dilapidated campsite, where I had lived for the past year, to seek medical help? How did I end up in a psychiatric hospital, listening to the screams of a patient in the locked ward at three o'clock in the morning?

Dr Satoshi wanted to know how it all began, so I showed him the scenario I had written to set the scene for the experiment.

'So let me get this right,' Dr Satoshi said. 'This wasn't meant to be a prediction. It was just a kind of fiction, right?'

I nodded. 'All the volunteers were supposed to read it before they arrived,' I said. 'Then we would continue the story, not by imagining what would happen next, but by acting it out in the real world.'

Dr Satoshi began reading out loud: '"At the dawn of the twenty-first century, most people in Britain assumed that life would continue much as it had done for the previous few decades. People would continue to get richer, live longer, and buy fancier electronic gadgets. They would continue to drive cars, work in offices, earn money, and buy their food in supermarkets. Although this way of life was only a few decades old, it seemed as timeless and permanent as the sun and the moon."'

He paused and looked at me. 'You write well. But I can detect a note of scepticism.' He smiled, and continued.

'"A few voices warned that this sense of permanence was an illusion, that infinite economic growth on a finite planet was impossible, that global warming and the looming energy crisis would soon put an end to the consumer-friendly economy. But few people took any notice. Academics discussed the possibility of economic collapse in comfortably upholstered leather armchairs, and politicians commissioned lengthy reports recommending policies that they had no intention of implementing. And the vast mass of ordinary people went on driving cars, working in offices, earning money, and buying their food in supermarkets."'

Dr Satoshi paused again. 'So you saw yourself as one of the few people who could see what was coming?' he asked. 'A lone voice crying in the wilderness?'

I grimaced at how grandiose that sounded. 'Yes,' I said, my cheeks reddening with embarrassment.

Dr Satoshi continued reading. '"Then the power cuts began. They started as an occasional annoyance, but it wasn't long before the electricity companies were having to schedule them so that people could at least plan for the current being switched off. Sales of emergency generators boomed, at least among those who could still afford such things. Those who couldn't just used candles, and sat around talking.

'"Cold showers were harder to adapt to, and many people preferred to stay dirty for longer. They had to wash their clothes by hand too, as washing machines were not very effective without hot water, and used too much electricity anyway. People became much smellier, and head lice began to spread rapidly. Duvets became infested with bedbugs, and the health system began to creak under the weight of so many cases of pneumonia. As rubbish collection became increasingly infrequent, rotting food and other waste began to pile up at street corners, and soon there were outbreaks of typhoid and cholera in London and New York."'

Dr Satoshi looked up from the printout. 'Your fictional scenario is quite convincing.'

I muttered a barely audible thank you. It no longer seemed very plausible to me.

'"And still most people failed to see that they were living through the beginnings of a catastrophe. Every day on the radio an array of experts could be heard claiming that a return to prosperity was just around the corner, and suggesting policy initiatives that would turn the economy around.

'"Then came Hurricane Gina. When it hit New York, on 30 September 2012, it did much more than make a lot of people and companies homeless. The insurance market was overwhelmed by the claims, and the resulting financial panic spread from one stock market to another like forest fire."

'Why did you choose that date?' Dr Satoshi asked. 'Does it have any special significance?'

I tried to think. 'It's the day after my birthday,' I said. 'And 2012 is when the Maya thought the world would end.'

Dr Satoshi looked at me for a moment, and then continued reading. '"Global supply chains snapped. Panic buying ensued, and within a day there was nothing left on the supermarket shelves. Looters took to the streets, and the army was deployed in all the major cities. But the soldiers were ill prepared for keeping martial law in their own country, and the trickle of desertions soon became a flood.

'"Everyone began to flee the cities – mostly on foot, as petrol quickly ran out. Most of the refugees did not get very far. Unaccustomed to sleeping outdoors or even camping, the cold weather put paid to thousands. Those who survived the frosty nights grew weak with hunger and disease.

'"All that seems a long time ago now. Today, in the year 2025, things have calmed down a lot. There are still some people living in the cities, but on the whole they aren't nice places to be. The only way to make a reasonable living there is by prostitution, drug-dealing, or protection rackets. Those who aren't involved in these lucrative trades struggle to make ends meet. They pull the copper out of the walls and rip out sinks and pipework to swap for food on street corners. They would love to move out to the country, but they know it's too late for that now – those who already live there don't look kindly on incomers. In fact, they have a nasty habit of killing them."'

Dr Satoshi raised his eyebrows. 'I thought your project was called the Utopia Experiment? That doesn't sound very utopian!'

'Go on,' I muttered. 'Read the last bit.'

He drew a deep breath, and went on.

'"Back in the first decade of the twenty-first century, before the crash, some of the few people who saw the writing on the wall got together and started preparing for the challenging times ahead. They set up self-sufficient communities in rural areas far enough away from the major cities to avoid the first wave of refugees. They taught themselves many old crafts that had been widespread before the Industrial Revolution, but which had largely died out in the twentieth century, such as weaving and smelting. They also learned to defend themselves against attacks by hostile strangers. And they began to store up cultural artefacts – books, music, works of art – to preserve for posterity, like secular equivalents of the European monasteries that preserved the great books of classical antiquity throughout the Dark Ages, and so enabled future generations to enjoy these ancient treasures.

'"One of those communities was called the Utopia Experiment. Nowadays, those of us who live here simply call it Utopia. It's not quite as ironic a name as it might first appear. For what we've discovered is that, in many ways, things are better now than they were before the crash – at least, they are for those of us who are lucky enough to live out here in the countryside. The air is much cleaner for one thing, and the wildlife has made a comeback. People have a lot more time to spend with their children, and neighbours are always helping each other out. And all that walking around and manual labour means that people are a lot fitter than they used to be. You certainly don't see any fat people any more. We like to think that the crash gave some people a second chance, an opportunity to escape from the awful state we'd got ourselves into in the late twentieth century."'

Dr Satoshi put down the printout and drew another deep breath.

'Well, that's some story!' he said. 'You are quite a writer.'

'I'll never be able to write again!' I blurted out. I could still hardly concentrate long enough to read more than a few sentences at a time, let alone write a coherent paragraph. Whenever I tried to note down my thoughts, I would lose track of what I was thinking after a single sentence, and my handwriting was a spidery scrawl.

'Nonsense; I couldn't have written this!' exclaimed Dr Satoshi, waving another printout at me. It was one of my academic papers, which he had downloaded from my website and read that morning. I was impressed by the time he was taking to understand me.

But I didn't believe him. I was convinced my academic career was at an end.

'If this had happened to you later in life,' Dr Satoshi continued, 'then things would look a lot bleaker. But you are forty years old. You have another twenty-five years to build up your savings before you retire. You can do it.'

It would mean starting again, from scratch. I had sold my house to pay for the Utopia Experiment, and I had nothing left apart from a few boxes of books that were currently sitting in a rusty shipping container in a muddy field.

'Look,' said Dr Satoshi. 'I see a lot of people from pretty poor backgrounds. I know that they will probably stay poor for the rest of their lives. When they are old, they will spend what little money they have playing bingo or drinking in their local pub. They don't have a problem with that. That vision doesn't hold any fear for them. But you would hate that. That's not the world you come from.'

I appreciated his honesty. It wasn't the kind of thing I imagined a psychiatrist would or should say. It certainly wasn't very politically correct. But it happened to fit very well with my way of thinking. The image of my older self eking out his last days in some cockney boozer, rubbing shoulders with badly spoken drunks and geriatric bingo players, put the fear of god in me. I would do anything to avoid that fate. I simply had to get well again.

'It is just as well you came here when you did. You have had a lucky escape.'

At the time, I didn't really understand what Dr Satoshi meant by those words. But it is clear to me now that I was unwell, not just mentally, but physically too. I was skinny and malnourished, dirty and unkempt.

'For the moment, I'm just going to put you back on citalopram.'

That was an antidepressant I'd been given when I was depressed before. It worked then. But then I hadn't been nearly so bad. I had managed to keep doing my job throughout the illness. And a few months later I was better, and came off the pills.

'We'll put you on forty milligrams a day and see how you get on.'

Twice my previous dosage. I hoped it would be enough.

'But tell me more about how the whole idea first came to you. The scenario is interesting, but why did you write it in the first place? When did you first think about setting up such a strange experiment?'

2. MEXICO

The idea for the Utopia Experiment first came to me in September 2005, while I was in Mexico. I had come at the invitation of the British Council to give a series of talks about robotics. The talks were informal affairs, held in cafes around Mexico City and Monterrey, with the aim of encouraging popular engagement with science and technology. I described my attempts to build robots with emotions, and tried to provoke debate about the benefits and dangers of artificial intelligence. Then, when all the talks were over, I took a flight to the Yucatán peninsula, to spend a week exploring Maya ruins.

I landed in Mérida, the largest city in the Yucatán. Founded by the Spanish conquistadores in 1542 on the site of an old Maya settlement, it still retains much of the old colonial charm that has been largely erased by modernity in Mexico City. You can even see some of the carved stones from the original Maya temples set in the walls of the main cathedral, as if the old gods still lingered on, unbowed by the weight of the Catholic statues above them. The genes, too, survive; Mérida has the highest percentage of indigenous people of any large city in Mexico, with over half of the inhabitants being of Maya descent. Their brown faces with beak-like noses, their colourful clothes and stocky bodies all mark them out from the paler descendants of the Spanish invaders, who are still far richer and taller and more powerful today, five centuries after they first arrived to plunder the New World.

As I wandered around the quiet streets, peering into the white buildings with their high ceilings and cool interiors, a young man came up to me and asked me where I was from.

'I'm from England,' I said.

'Oh, England! You are Englishman!' He smiled. 'You want to see traditional Mexican clothes? I take you to shop with good prices.'

The first rule of buying stuff abroad is never to do it on your first day. Take your time, stroll around, look at what's on offer and compare the prices. If you shop around you soon discover that the same item can be bought somewhere else for ten times less than in the first shop you entered.

'To hell with that,' I thought. 'I'm on holiday! Everything is so damn cheap here anyway. Why not go and see what this guy has to show?'

So I followed the young man down a couple of side streets, through a large wooden doorway, into the courtyard of a colonial house, where several old Maya women sat weaving and embroidering in the shade of the archways.

He introduced me to one of the women.

'Hello,' she smiled. 'What is your name?'

'Dylan. *¿Cómo se llama usted?*'

'Ah, you speak Spanish!' she exclaimed. '*¡Qué bien! Yo me llamo María.* Would you like to see some traditional Mexican clothes?'

She led me through one of the archways into a large room, where the clothes hung densely from every nook and cranny, making a kind of textile maze. There were brightly coloured blankets with zigzag designs, crisp white shirts with fine tiny pleats, thick grey woollen ponchos, pale brown sombreros made of straw and black ones made of felt, and, at the back of the room, shelf upon shelf of neatly folded hammocks.

'Maybe you would like to try on a *guayabera*?' asked Maria.

She took a shirt off its coat hanger and handed it to me. It was a brownish off-white in colour and slightly rough to the touch, in a pleasant kind of way, but not at all heavy. It didn't feel like cotton.

'What's it made of?' I asked.

'Sisal. Very good quality.'

Sisal is a coarse fibre made from a species of agave, a vaguely cactus-like plant with thick, fleshy, waxen leaves that shoot up from the ground and end in a fierce-looking sharp spike. The leaves are crushed and beaten until only fibres remain, which are then dried and brushed before weaving. Clothes made from sisal help to ward off mosquitoes, since they retain some of the agave's natural insecticides. They are also very cool and lightweight, making them ideal for the hot Mexican climate.

I ended up buying not just the shirt but also a pair of matching baggy trousers, and a sombrero, also made of sisal. I thought I looked faintly ridiculous in this traditional Mexican garb, but Maria assured me I looked very handsome and dignified.

'Maybe you would like to try a hammock too?' she asked.

'I'm not sure I really want to buy a hammock right now,' I mumbled.

'Come on! Try! Try!'

Maria led me back out into the courtyard, where a hammock had magically been strung between the pillars of one of the archways that formed the perimeter. She gestured to me to lie down in it, and when I did she handed me a small wooden cup with a clear liquid inside.

'What's this?' I asked.

'Traditional Mexican drink. I think you like. Try!'

Gingerly, I took a small sip. Wow! It was strong. It tasted like tequila, and left a burning sensation in my throat. I gasped for breath.

Maria laughed. 'You like?'

I tried to speak but my voice was hoarse. I nodded politely, and took another sip to show willing. And then another.

I lay back in the hammock and closed my eyes. It felt

very comfortable, as if my body was melting into it. A warm sensation spread over my limbs, and I pictured myself in a few years' time, reclining in the same hammock in some Mediterranean villa that, by some stroke of good luck, I now owned. Life was good.

I bought the hammock too, of course.

The next day I took a bus to Uxmal, an ancient Maya city about sixty kilometres south of Mérida that flourished between 600 and 1000 CE. Our bus arrived mid-morning, and the sun was already fierce. I was grateful for my sombrero, and wished I had also donned my sisal shirt and trousers, instead of my customary T-shirt and jeans, which were soon clinging to my body, damp with humidity and sweat. But I forgot all about my discomfort when I saw the great Pyramid of the Magician, an imposing grey stone building standing over thirty-five metres tall. It is unlike other Mayan pyramids in having slightly rounded sides and an elliptical base. The sides are also steeper than usual, and it was with some trepidation that I climbed to the top, panting in the heat. When I finally reached the temple that stood at the summit, I turned round and surveyed the rest of the site.

I remember a feeling of melancholy coming over me as I pictured the bustling crowds who must have once thronged the streets and squares below, a thousand years before. In the distance, where once there would have been fields full of maize and beans, all I could see now was the green canopy of the jungle, stretching in all directions, punctuated only here and there by the peaks of distant pyramids, marking the sites of other lost cities.

My reverie was interrupted by our guide, who sat down next to me and asked me where I was from.

'I'm from England,' I replied.

'Far away?'

'Yes, very far away. Where are you from?'

He mentioned the name of a place I had never heard of, but I nodded as if I knew exactly where it was.

'What do you do back home?'

How do you explain to someone who may never have even *seen* a robot that you are trying to build robots that have emotions?

'I'm trying to build machines that have feelings,' I said.

My guide looked puzzled. 'Why?' he asked.

I drew a deep breath.

'Well, many people think that machines will become more and more intelligent over the coming years. They will become like people, and they will live with us in our houses, like servants or even friends. And that means they will have to be able to recognize our emotions, and maybe even express their own feelings too.'

The guide nodded, and looked down at his feet for a few moments.

'But why do people want machines like that?'

That was a question I had been asking myself recently too. When I had first become interested in the possibility of emotional robots, I was so fascinated by the very idea that I hadn't paused to consider such practical questions as what such machines might be used for, and why companies might bother to manufacture them. But now I was actually trying to build an emotional robot, those questions were becoming more pressing – not least because I had to justify my project when I was applying for funding and talking to journalists. And I found it increasingly hard to give a sensible answer. I wanted to build emotional robots because I thought it was damn good fun. But did they have any real use?

I trotted out my standard answer, even though I didn't find it very convincing.

'Well, one reason might be to provide companions for elderly people,' I said. 'A lot of elderly people in my country are very lonely, and don't have anyone to talk to. So they might appreciate a robot companion, if it was sensitive and sympathetic.'

'But why can't the old people keep each other company?' asked the guide.

Now it was my turn to look down at my shoes. He had seen the same flaw as me: why seek a technological fix for a social problem? Is the answer to loneliness really just to make more gadgets? I imagined a block of flats, each with a single elderly person inside, and a robot companion sitting next to each one. It was not a happy thought.

But instead of conceding the point, I tried to battle on, and suggested that perhaps a robot companion might in some ways be even better than a human one. As I spoke, though, I could see the expression of puzzlement on the guide's face deepen, and it struck me that not only were our two worlds separated by a cultural chasm, but that my world was perhaps rather pointless and self-indulgent in the greater scheme of things. This man could barely make ends meet. And I was building robots.

Uxmal was one of the last great Maya cities to fall into ruin. It was still flourishing in the ninth century CE, when crisis was sweeping the southern lowlands in what is present-day Guatemala, and populations there plummeted as city after city was abandoned. But eventually Uxmal fell silent too.

The reasons for the Maya collapse are complex, but climate change seems to have played an important role. There is evidence of an intense drought lasting two hundred years, and this was compounded by deforestation. As the cities expanded, more farmland was needed to feed the growing population, and the transformation of forest into cropland led to reduced transpiration and thus to less rainfall. Crops failed, famine ravaged the cities, and a bloody civil war erupted as the people turned on the ruling castes, who seemed to have lost favour with Chaac, the rain god.

This picture of a growing population outstripping its food supply seems to fit well with the ideas of the British clergyman Thomas Malthus. In his 1798 *Essay on the*

Principle of Population, he argued that there is a hard limit to the number of people that can be sustained by a given amount of land. Today, ecologists talk about the earth's natural carrying capacity, and how disaster looms as humans exceed it. The basic idea is the same. Sooner or later, Malthus argued, a growing population will always reach a point where it can no longer grow enough food to feed itself. And then something must happen to cut the population down to size. Perhaps 'sickly seasons, epidemics, pestilence, and plague [will] advance in terrific array, and sweep off their thousands and tens of thousands'. And if these disasters do not bring the population back down to a viable size, 'gigantic inevitable famine stalks in the rear, and with one mighty blow levels the population with the food of the world'.

The parallels between the Maya collapse and our current global predicament are clear. Just as the Maya grew too numerous for the carrying capacity of their environment, so the global population was threatening to grow beyond the carrying capacity of the earth itself. In 2005, when I climbed that pyramid in Uxmal, there were six and a half billion people on the planet. That was forecast to rise to over nine billion by 2050. How would we be able to feed those extra billions when there was already famine in many parts of the globe? If a great civilization like that of the Maya could implode, could the modern world fall prey to the same fate?

There are, of course, some big differences between the world of the Maya and our own. For one thing, our civilization is global, so if one part of the world gets into trouble, the rest of the world can help. The Maya, on the other hand, were isolated by the lack of ocean-going vessels.

Globalization also means, however, that trouble can quickly be exported. A new strain of bird-flu emerging from the markets of Guangdong could become a global epidemic. An earthquake in Tokyo would send shock-waves throughout the world's financial system as insurers liquidated their assets to settle all the claims.

The hyper-efficient supply chains that bring cheap food to our tables are also increasingly vulnerable to local shocks. When goods are shipped on demand and inventory is reduced to a minimum, one broken link can disrupt the entire chain. A supermarket stocks perhaps enough food for three meals for each consumer in its catchment area. Those three meals are all that stand between civilization and anarchy.

If the idea of our civilization collapsing seems outlandish, then no doubt the idea would have seemed equally crazy to the Maya at their heyday. The crowds who once thronged the streets of Uxmal would surely have scoffed at the suggestion that, within a few years, those same streets would be empty and silent.

So when I sat atop that pyramid and felt overcome by images of the Maya collapse, it whispered of the fragility and impermanence of my own high-tech world. Pictures of Hurricane Katrina were still fresh in my mind. When a single storm could unleash hordes of looters and federal troops onto the streets of the most advanced country on earth, it was not hard to see a parallel in the ruins of Uxmal.

The Maya did not die out when their civilization collapsed. Millions perished, but some survived by retreating into the jungle. If a global catastrophe put an end to our modern world, something similar would no doubt happen to us. The survivors would abandon the cities and eke out a living in places where they could grow or catch their own food. This would not be so hard for those in developing countries, where there are still many who live off the land. The Maya even figured out a way to make clothes from spiky plants! They lived without modern technology for thousands of years, and some still do, in the little villages that dot the jungle in the Yucatán peninsula. But what about the people in advanced economies, where only a tiny proportion of the population knows anything about farming? How would the refugees from New York or London cope in the aftermath of a global catastrophe?

These were the questions that began to sprout in my mind in the days after my visit to Uxmal. As I travelled further east, and visited other ruined cities, I began to conceive of a kind of experiment that might provide some answers. Instead of trying to imagine, from the comfort of my armchair, what life might be like if civilization collapsed, I would act it out, with the help of some volunteers. We would grow our own food, make our own clothes, and do everything else necessary to survive, without any of the resources of our modern high-tech world. But it wouldn't simply be another hippy commune or Walden Pond – it would be an exercise in collaborative fiction, continually informed by a scenario of global collapse, which we would develop further as we played it out in the real world.

By the time I reached Tulum, the site of an ancient Maya city on the east coast of the Yucatán peninsula, the experiment was no longer a fanciful idea but a definite plan of action. Though somewhat smaller than Uxmal, Tulum once served as a port, and the ruins stand atop small cliffs, looking out over the Caribbean Sea. It was one of the last cities inhabited by the Maya, and managed to survive for several decades after the Spanish first arrived in Mexico, until the population finally succumbed to European viruses.

I found a beach hut to rent for a couple of days, a very simple structure – a circular whitewashed wall, probably made of brick, with a large straw cone on top. A makeshift wooden door allowed access, and inside there was nothing but a camp bed and a small wooden table. The floor was merely the sandy beach on which the hut stood.

I eased my rucksack off my back and let it drop onto the bed. It was around midday and the sunlight filtered through the straw roof, giving just enough light to unpack my things. There were my new Mexican shirt and trousers, my new hammock, a couple of T-shirts, some socks and underwear, swimming trunks, a book or two, and toiletries. These were all the things in the world I had with me now, and yet they seemed quite enough. I felt gloriously unencumbered, and yearned to live like this forever, with almost no possessions and in the simplest kind of abode.

I changed into my swimming trunks and wandered down to the sea. It was warm and friendly, and after paddling out a little I turned over and let myself float with my eyes closed. I felt the warm sun on my face and the gentle motion of the waves as my body rose and fell with the swell. It was paradise.

Later, as the sun began to go down, I spotted a small group of people making a barbecue higher up on the beach. They were about five young Mexican men, all in shorts and nothing else on, their muscular bodies glowing with golden tans. I walked over to say hi, but when the young man tending to the smoking fish looked up he did a double take.

'Were you in Mérida recently?'

I nodded, puzzled by his reaction. I certainly didn't remember meeting him there.

Then he turned to his friends and said, in Spanish: 'That's the guy who paid a fortune for the clothes in Mérida!'

A peel of laughter rippled round the group. The young man looked back at me, smiling broadly, without the slightest suspicion that I had understood his remark.

So, word had somehow travelled all the way from Mérida to the coast about this gullible gringo. Had I really overpaid *that* much for those clothes, to become the subject of such far-flung gossip? I was frankly spooked by the idea. But only for a short while. Before too long, I had drifted back into a whimsical and carefree mood that remained with me for the rest of my time in Mexico.

Relaxing on that warm beach, the idea of post-apocalyptic living didn't seem all that bad. True, the collapse itself would be dreadful, but for those who survived, the simpler way of life they would be forced to adopt might well have certain advantages over the technological one that had preceded it. It might be positively utopian.

To call something utopian is, of course, not entirely positive. The connotation of a perfect society is offset by that of a hopelessly impractical ideal. And it was probably the latter meaning that Thomas More had in mind when he coined the term *Utopia* in his 1516 book of the same title. For he derived the word from the Greek οὐ (not) and τόπος (place), meaning literally *nowhere*. The implication is that while we might dream of a perfect society, we will never find it in this world.

And yet, despite this clear warning, there have been no end of idealists who have taken More's book as an exhortation to turn his fantasy into a reality. The very first of these was a Spanish churchman by the name of Vasco de Quiroga, and the place he chose to build his Utopia was, as it happens, in Mexico. A mere two decades after the publication of More's book, Quiroga used it as the blueprint for a commune he established on the outskirts of Mexico City.

Here, in the vicinity of Lake Pátzcuaro, the Indians would be taught not just the Christian religion, but also a variety of arts and crafts, and the fundamentals of self-government. Like many utopian communities ever since, the settlements created by Quiroga also had elements of primitive socialism: each person worked six hours a day and contributed on an equal basis to the common welfare.

It was strangely appropriate, then, that the idea for the Utopia Experiment should have occurred to me in Mexico. And yet, there was also something surreal about those sun-soaked days in Tulum. Everything seemed so magical, so dreamy. I would later wonder what was in that drink the woman gave me in Mérida. Was it some kind of hallucinogenic substance, or some magic potion perhaps, that made me so willing to part with my money, to give up everything I had even, and live a life without possessions? Was I under some kind of spell when I first came up with the idea for the Utopia Experiment?

Back in England, the weather was dark and gloomy, and I began to put my vague plan into action. The first task was to find a suitable location. What sort of place would the survivors of a global catastrophe find refuge in? If the collapse was due in part to climate change, the places favoured by the old climate might become inhospitable.

According to some forecasts, the south of England would become increasingly dry and infertile, but rainfall would still be plentiful in the Scottish Highlands, and rising temperatures there would mean that it would be more conducive to agriculture. Perhaps a few far-sighted people from the big cities would head north before the shit hit the fan, and prepare for the coming collapse by growing their own food and weaning themselves off the technology that would soon disappear. Just as a few Maya survived the collapse of their civilization by retreating into the jungle, so a few refugees from London and Edinburgh might eke out a living in the Scottish Highlands.

As it happened, I had an old friend from the Highlands who might be able to help. I had met Romay at Southampton University in 1987. While we were students she had often talked about going back to the Highlands, and in the year 2000 she did just that, buying and renovating the old farmhouse where she had spent her childhood. Her brother had inherited the farmland around it, on which he now raised some of the best beef cattle in Scotland.

Nervously, I picked up the phone and dialled Romay's number.

'Do you think your brother would let me use a couple of acres of land for an experiment?' I asked.

Romay hesitated. Her brother, Alastair, was a no-nonsense, sensible kind of a man, and not the most likely candidate to allow strangers to live on his land to conduct an experiment in post-apocalyptic living. But her enthusiasm for my idea got the better of her.

'Yes,' she said. 'I think you could probably persuade him. And I know the perfect place.'

A few weeks later I travelled to Scotland for a week to get a better idea of the territory. I had been here many times before, but never really paid much attention to the topography of the land that lay between Romay's farmhouse and Alastair's farm, which lay on the northern shores of the Black Isle, north of Inverness. A stream cut through the fields and formed a small valley, densely overgrown with trees and bracken. Here, with the surrounding farmland out of sight, you suddenly felt very far from civilization. This was the site Romay suggested.

As I arrived the last rays of sunshine were glinting off the snow-covered peaks in the distance. Romay greeted me with her usual enthusiasm. She was in her late forties, with tousled brown hair flecked with grey, and dark brown eyes that twinkled mischievously when she smiled. But she also had a toughness born of years of fending for herself and bringing up two children on her own. Now, back in the land of her birth, she seemed in her element striding through the muddy fields in her green Wellington boots, as she took me round the site of the future Utopia.

There was a small waterfall we might use to generate electricity. Slopes either side of the stream might be good to terrace for fruit trees and berry bushes. At one point the valley widened to form a flat area either side of the water that might provide a suitable site to set up our camp.

Above the valley lay a large potato shed with stone walls and a roof of rusty corrugated iron. There were a few holes in the roof that would need patching to make it waterproof, and we would need to put some doors in the gaping holes where the wind now blew, but apart from that the shed was in pretty good shape. This, Romay suggested, could be a communal eating and cooking area.

Near the potato shed was an acre of scrubland where we could grow our crops and keep a few pigs and chickens. The land was stony and would need a lot of preparation before we could plant anything. But the soil was rich and dark, and although it was north-facing, the slope was gentle enough to catch a good deal of the intermittent sunshine.

But I had no idea about farming. The only thing I had ever grown was a cannabis plant, and that was more out of curiosity than for any practical purposes. I was the least green-fingered person you could imagine. The idea of me tilling the land, and planting seedlings, and harvesting the crops, would have seemed ludicrous to my friends and family. But at that time I had heroic visions of becoming a horny-handed son of toil, labouring away like some diligent yeoman in a Thomas Hardy novel. I was blissfully unaware of how ill-suited I was to that way of life.

3. ROBOTS

When I got back from my trip to Scotland, I set up a page on my website headed *An experiment in Utopia*. I announced that I was setting up a novel kind of community based on three main ideas:

1. It will be a LEARNING COMMUNITY – each member must have a distinctive skill or area of knowledge that they can teach to the others.
2. It will be a WORKING COMMUNITY – no money is required from the members, but all must contribute by working.
3. It will be strictly TIME-LIMITED. This is not an attempt to found an ongoing community. The experiment will last 18 months. Members may stay for up to three months, but may also come for as little as two weeks.

    In a word, think of a cross between Plato's Academy and *The Beach*.

The reference to Plato may sound grandiose, but his Academy was really just an olive grove outside the city walls of ancient Athens where his friends and followers would gather to study and discuss philosophy. It was this high-minded but informal atmosphere that I wanted to recreate.

The Beach tells of another Utopia. The protagonist of Alex Garland's blockbuster novel is a young backpacker who discovers a hidden beach in Thailand, where a small community of young people from all over the world live together amidst idyllic surroundings. At first everything goes well, and our hero thinks he has found paradise. But, eventually, everything ends in disaster.

For some reason the ominous implications of citing *The Beach* as inspiration for my experiment escaped my mind at the time. Nor did I put much thought into how I would select the volunteers. I simply asked them to send me a two-hundred-word email telling me who they were, and what they could offer the community.

I made no attempt to promote the webpage or tell anyone the announcement was there. The only way you could find it was by following a link from my home page. I was curious to see if the first people who followed that link would share it, and whether it might take on a momentum of its own.

Sure enough, within a few days, the first volunteers were beginning to contact me. It started off as a trickle, but before long I had received several hundred applications to join the experimental community. And, despite my friends' predictions, they weren't all hippies in their twenties. With ages ranging from eighteen to sixty-seven, and a roughly equal mix of men and women, they came from a wide range of backgrounds. They included an ex-Royal Marine turned shoemaker, a computer programmer passionate about vegetables, a retired schoolteacher who had spent time with the Inuit, a journalist from India, a graffiti artist from Belfast, and a Cambridge graduate who offered to be the community musician.

There was nothing about the end of the world in the original outline I posted online; it wasn't until a few months later that I wrote the fictional scenario Dr Satoshi read. I can't remember why I chose not to reveal that aspect of the experiment at this stage. Maybe I was still sufficiently sane to realize how crazy it sounded. Maybe I didn't want to give away too much.

Nevertheless, several of the first people to apply made it clear they were already thinking along similar lines. One of those was Agric.

A self-employed computer technician in his early fifties, he lived in Slough and grew his own vegetables – but he was planning to sell his house and become a nomad.

In his first email to me, after explaining why he would like to volunteer, Agric concluded with a 'heads up' about the dire consequences of peak oil.

Peak oil is the moment when global oil production starts to decline. Working for Shell in the 1950s, a geologist called Marion King Hubbert suggested that oil production would follow a bell-shaped curve. At first the rate of production is very low, but then it begins to increase rapidly until it reaches a peak, stabilizes, and then declines equally rapidly.

Agric was not alone in thinking peak oil was imminent. I soon found out that it was a common belief among doomers – people who believe that a global catastrophe will happen within the next few years. Doomers attribute the catastrophe to a variety of possible causes, from global warming to financial crises, but the end of cheap oil is a pretty popular choice. And when one considers how central oil is to our modern technological civilization, it is easy to see why.

At the other end of the optimism scale from the doomers are the boomers, or cornucopians, who believe that continued technological progress will solve all our problems and lead to an ever-increasing standard of living.

For a long time I had counted myself firmly among the cornucopians. I was confident that humanity was headed for the kind of techno-utopia envisaged by science fiction writers like Arthur C. Clarke, who famously wrote that 'any sufficiently advanced technology is indistinguishable from magic'. And I desperately wanted to be part of that future, to make it happen.

Enthused by the promises of artificial intelligence, I had managed to land a job at one of the best-equipped robotics labs in the world – the Bristol Robotics Laboratory (then known as the Intelligent Autonomous Systems

Lab). Like most of the other researchers I met there, I started off with grand ambitions to build robots that would be able to run around, hold intelligent conversations, and free people from dull, dirty and dangerous jobs. Of course, I knew that there would be big challenges in designing such advanced technology, but I hadn't realized that the biggest one of all would be energy. Energy is the dirty secret of robotics.

Artificial intelligence still has a long way to go before it rivals human intelligence, but it has already achieved some impressive feats: beating world champions at chess, and more mundane but actually more demanding tasks, such as driving cars and recognizing faces. But all the most advanced intelligence won't get you very far if you run out of energy, and most robots run out of energy very quickly. That's because they rely on batteries, and batteries, despite all the progress with the lithium-ion devices that power our mobile phones, are still terribly inefficient. At least, they are when compared with the biological mechanisms that power living creatures like ants and humans. Think of how small an ant is – and how long it can walk around, carrying several times its own body-weight. In order to get a robotic ant to do that, you would have to give it a battery much bigger than itself. But then it would need a lot more energy to carry that battery around, so you would have to give it an even bigger battery, and so on.

After a few months in Bristol it struck me that, in this sense (and in many others), robots were rather like human societies. Their intelligence outstripped their energy – they could perform all sorts of amazing intellectual endeavours, but they kept running up against an energy deficit, and needed to find ever more resources to fill it. Many societies collapsed in the past because their energy requirements began to outstrip their energy resources.

The Maya are a case in point, but other examples are not hard to find. Easter Island is a small and very remote patch of land in the Pacific Ocean. When a small group of Polynesian settlers arrived there eight hundred years ago, it was covered in trees – perhaps as many as sixteen million of them, some towering a hundred feet tall. The settlers proceeded to burn down the woods to free up farmland, and began to multiply. Eventually the population grew to perhaps fifteen thousand, and they ran out of trees. Without trees, the islanders couldn't build any more canoes to go fishing, and soil erosion ate away at their farmland.

By the time Captain James Cook visited in 1774, there were only a few hundred islanders left, living hand to mouth. All that remained of the once proud civilization their ancestors had created were the tall stone statues for which Easter Island is famous today. And many of them had been torn down by rival clans, who had turned on each other as their society collapsed.

I began to think the global village was in the same situation as the Maya and the inhabitants of Easter Island. For years, our civilization had been powering itself with fossil fuels – especially oil – and we kept needing more and more. But sooner or later we would run out. And that, as Agric would later remind me constantly, would mark the beginning of the end.

But in another sense, human societies were very unlike the robots in my lab. A lot of our research there focused on something known as 'swarm intelligence'. This involved taking a lot of very simple robots and programming them to work as a team. The idea was that, even though each robot was quite stupid on its own, a kind of collective intelligence – a hive mind – would emerge when they worked together to achieve a common goal. Human societies, it struck me, were just the opposite. Individually, people are very intelligent creatures. But in society a kind of collective stupidity seems to emerge spontaneously. The Scottish journalist Charles Mackay famously called it 'the madness of crowds' in an 1841 book that chronicled such follies as economic bubbles, the Crusades and witch-hunts. 'Men,' he wrote, 'go mad in herds, while they only recover their senses slowly, and one by one.'

The global village was going mad too, it seemed to me. Despite all the protestations of sensible individuals about the dangers of climate change, the world as a whole seemed incapable of doing anything about it. But surely there was a way to form a sane community, one not overtaken by groupthink and delusion? My Utopia Experiment would be an attempt to create just such a society, in miniature.

*

Many doomers actually look forward to the collapse of modern civilization. They know that billions of people will die, but they think the world is due for a correction, just like an economic bubble that is bound to burst. In the aftermath, however, the survivors will have the chance to rebuild a more humane kind of society, untroubled by the many ills of industrialization.

In this world view, the coming collapse becomes a kind of secular apocalypse, a naturalistic equivalent to the Tribulation of Christian theology, in which many people will perish in disasters, famine and war. Just as the Tribulation is a punishment meted out by God in response to our sins, so the collapse of modern civilization is the vengeance of Mother Earth for polluting the environment and a punishment for overconsumption. And just as the Tribulation will be followed by a thousand years of peace and prosperity, the collapse will be followed by a return to a blissful pre-industrial way of life.

There seems to be something universal about this storyline. Revolutionary socialism and fascism are heirs to this tradition just as much as Waco and Jonestown. Peak oil is just the latest incarnation of this pan-cultural impulse.

It's easy to understand why those with little stake in the current world order, those who have been left behind by technological progress, might be especially susceptible to the millennial impulse. There are also, however, a number of people working at the cutting edge who have converted to this seductive creed at the height of their technical prowess. I was working in a leading robotics lab when I underwent my conversion. Before me there were other, far more eminent scientists who trod the same path.

Take Bill Joy for example. The co-founder of Sun Microsystems was a legendary programmer, writing pioneering software in the late seventies and early eighties. So it came as quite a shock to the tech world when, in the April 2000 issue of *Wired* magazine, Joy expressed deep concerns over the increasing power of computers and other new technologies. 'Our most powerful 21st-century technologies,' he declared, 'are threatening to make humans an endangered species.'

In the *Wired* article, Joy traced his unease to a conversation he had had with Ray Kurzweil a few years before. Kurzweil has pioneered many developments in artificial intelligence, from optical character recognition to music synthesizers, and in 2012 he became Director of Engineering at Google. He is also a leading transhumanist, who hopes that future developments in technology will radically transform human nature for the better. When Kurzweil told Joy back in 1998 that humans 'were going to become robots or fuse with robots or something like that,' Joy was taken aback:

While I had heard such talk before, I had always felt sentient robots were in the realm of science fiction. But now, from someone I respected, I was hearing a strong argument that they were a near-term possibility [. . .] I already knew that new technologies like genetic engineering and nanotechnology were giving us the power to remake the world, but a realistic and imminent scenario for intelligent robots surprised me.

In the hotel bar, Kurzweil gave Joy a partial preprint of his forthcoming book *The Age of Spiritual Machines*, which outlined the technological Utopia he foresaw. On reading it, Joy's sense of unease only intensified; he felt sure Kurzweil was understating the dangers, underestimating the probability of a bad outcome along this path. He found himself most troubled by a passage detailing a dystopian scenario in which all work is done by vast, highly organized systems of machines, and no human effort is necessary. At that point, the fate of the human race would be at the mercy of the machines.

It might be argued that the human race would never be foolish enough to hand over all the power to the machines. But we are suggesting neither that the human race would voluntarily turn power over to the machines, nor that the machines would willfully seize power. What we do suggest is that the human race might easily permit itself to drift into a position of such dependence on the machines that it would have no practical choice but to accept all of the machines' decisions. As society and the problems that face it become more and more complex, and machines become more and more intelligent, people will let machines make more of their decisions for them, simply because machine-made decisions will bring better results than man-made ones. Eventually a stage may be reached at which the decisions necessary to keep the system running will be so complex that human beings will be incapable of making them intelligently. At that stage the machines will be in effective control. People won't be able to just turn the machines off, because they will be so dependent on them that turning them off would amount to suicide.

In Kurzweil's book, you don't discover until you turn the page that the author of this passage is Theodore Kaczynski, the notorious Unabomber, whose bombs killed three people during a seventeen-year terror campaign and wounded many others.

Kaczynski was a brilliant mathematician who resigned his job as an assistant professor at the University of California, Berkeley, just two years after receiving his PhD, and vanished. In 1971 he moved into a remote log cabin in Montana where he lived a simple life, without electricity or running water. In 1978 he began sending out mailbombs, targeting engineers, computer scientists and geneticists.

The Unabomber wrote his rambling 35,000-word manifesto on an old typewriter during the long years he spent alone in his cabin. In 1995 he wrote to several newspapers promising to end his bombing campaign if they printed it. After lengthy deliberations, the *New York Times* and the *Washington Post* agreed. By a curious twist of fate, that was Kaczynski's undoing. His brother read the published essay, recognized the writing style, and went to the FBI. The Unabomber was arrested the following year, and is now serving a life sentence at the federal supermax prison in Florence, Colorado.

One of Kaczynski's bombs had gravely injured Bill Joy's friend David Gelernter, a brilliant and visionary computer scientist. At one time, Joy felt that he could easily have been the Unabomber's next target. Nevertheless, when he read the extract from the Unabomber's manifesto in Kurzweil's book, Joy saw some merit in the reasoning. 'I felt compelled to confront it,' he would later write in his *Wired* article. Not long after the article was published, Joy decided he could no longer continue 'working to create tools which will enable the construction of the technology that may replace our species', and quit his job in Silicon Valley.

My first encounter with the Unabomber manifesto affected me just as deeply. In late 2005, shortly after my trip to Mexico, I visited my friend Nick Bostrom in Oxford. I had first met Nick eight years earlier, while we were both PhD students in the Philosophy Department at the London School of Economics. Now he had a fabulous job with perhaps the best job title I have ever seen: Director of the Future of Humanity Institute. Of course it would have been even more impressive without the final word.

Nick had written his doctoral dissertation about the doomsday argument, which purports to show that human extinction is likely to occur sooner rather than later. Now, five years on, he was still interested in the prospects for human extinction, and he was setting up a research programme to investigate the likelihood of a global catastrophe.

The night I went to have supper with Nick in his Oxford college was Halloween, and for once he didn't look out of place in his long black gown. As we chatted over a festive meal of turkey and cranberry sauce, I told him about my growing disenchantment with technology, and my plans for the Utopia Experiment. Nick was interested, but not particularly surprised.

'Have you read the Unabomber manifesto?' he asked nonchalantly.

I hadn't. In fact, I hadn't even heard of the Unabomber.

'You should definitely check it out,' said Nick.

Intrigued, I searched for the manifesto online as soon as I got home, and read it that very night. And right away, I was hooked.

The manifesto is a curious and erratic document. Some sections are eloquent and persuasive, while others merely rambling and adolescent. Nevertheless, I found it intoxicating, in a way that perhaps affected Bill Joy too. We were both working at the cutting edge of artificial intelligence when we first read it, and both had incipient doubts about the risks posed by that technology. We both felt complicit in creating the terrifying future the Unabomber prophesied, and we were fertile ground for his more extreme claims.

Part of the manifesto's attraction also lay, I now think, in the easy explanation it provided for my growing sense of malaise. For the past year or so I had been feeling increasingly out of sorts. In hindsight, I can see the tell-tale early warning signs of depression in the diary I kept, but they crept up on me so gradually that I didn't notice the subtle change I was undergoing. My mood darkened so slowly, that by the time night had fallen, I couldn't remember how things looked in the daylight.

The Unabomber gave me a convenient scapegoat for my ills. My angst had nothing to do with me; it was all society's fault. More specifically, it was the fault of the industrial-technological system, which robbed us of our autonomy, diminished our rapport with nature, and forced us 'to behave in ways that are increasingly remote from the natural pattern of human behavior'. It was hardly an original idea, and not one that had held any attraction for me before, but now the simple, stark language of the manifesto hypnotized me, and within a few days I was spouting Kaczynski's strange gospel as fervently as a religious convert. I had, as they might say today, been 'radicalized'. I did not conclude, as Kaczynski had done, that I should help bring on the collapse of civilization by killing computer scientists, but I did begin to look forward to the day when it would collapse of its own accord, and humanity could return to its pre-industrial past.

I can trace the development of these thoughts from the notes I made at the time in a black Moleskine notebook. Punctuating the various sketches for the Utopia Experiment are a series of entries recounting the story of a young monkey called Rousseau. Like his fellow monkeys, Rousseau doesn't realize that the cage he lives in is not his natural habitat, for he was born in captivity. But then he strikes up a conversation with a baboon in a nearby cage.

The baboon reveals to him that the source of all his low-level angst, his sense of anomie and alienation, is the fact that he is not living as nature intended.

'It's not natural to live in a cage, to be fed by human beings, to have no predators, to spend your days aimlessly shuffling around this enclosure,' says the baboon.

'Rubbish!' replies Rousseau. 'It feels perfectly natural to me.'

'That's because it is all you've ever known,' replies the baboon. 'But if it was perfectly natural, do you really think you would have these feelings of emptiness and purposelessness? Monkeys who are not born in cages never have these feelings. Their whole life makes sense to them. They never have these existential crises because they are just immersed in the business of living. They get hungry, they find food, they eat, and they rest and play – all without the slightest uneasy thought. They suffer and die too, of course, but without any worries about the meaning of it all ever crossing their minds.'

'Really?' exclaims the young monkey, half amused by this wonderful thought, half doubting that it could possibly be true.

'Sure,' says the baboon, 'let me show you.'

And so, together, they plan their escape from the zoo.

That little monkey was my alter ego, and the lab where I worked was feeling increasingly like a zoo. Not just because the robots we were building were all inspired by animals – we had robot rats and robots that ate flies – but because I felt like a caged animal myself. And it wasn't just the lab that felt like a cage, either. The whole modern world felt increasingly artificial, far removed from the natural habitat in which the human race evolved, out there in the scrubland of the African savannah.

I began to lose interest in the classes I was giving, and would leave my students to work on the tasks I assigned them while I sat silently in a corner, my head buried in the Unabomber's manifesto, or some other anti-technology tract. I now wonder what they made of all this. Did they ask themselves how this evangelist for artificial intelligence had turned into such a Luddite? Did they notice the full extent of my intellectual U-turn?

Perhaps they saw me in the same way as Nick Rosen, a documentary film-maker who came to interview me at the lab in the spring of 2006. Nick was researching a book about living off-grid, and had read about my plans for the Utopia Experiment online. A tall, slender man in his fifties with short dark hair and a relaxed gait, he arrived one afternoon with his tape recorder and note-book at the ready.

I greeted him at the reception desk and led him into the lab, a vast space with high ceilings, filled with strange-looking gizmos of all shapes and sizes.

'Let me give you a tour,' I said.

First I showed him our *pièce de résistance*, a small mobile robot that looked like a Frisbee on wheels, with a clear plastic box on top containing a slimy black liquid.

'This is our fly-eating robot!' I proudly announced.

Nick looked suitably impressed. 'How does it work?' he asked.

'You see that plastic box? Well, it's a microbial fuel cell. That black sludge contains lots of bacteria that can digest chitin. Chitin is what insect exoskeletons are made of. If we pop a few dead flies in this part, the bacteria will chew up the chitin, and electrons will be given off in the process. And these electrons can be used to generate an electric current, which powers the robot.'

'What does the robot do with the energy it gets from eating flies?' asked Nick.

'It moves, in search of more flies.'

'How fast does it move?'

'Oh, only a few centimetres an hour.'

'It's not exactly the Terminator, is it?' smiled Nick.

'No, of course not. I don't think the human race has to worry about being devoured by flesh-eating robots quite yet,' I laughed.

'But we might have to one day?'

I didn't reply. The nightmare scenarios that worried me these days didn't involve gruesome battles between humans and machines. They revolved around more subtle, but to my mind more plausible, scenarios, in which humans became so dependent on robots that they lost their autonomy. This was the future that worried the Unabomber, and now it worried me.

Next, I led Nick to another cubicle where a couple of my colleagues were fiddling around with little flexible filaments of plastic, and trying to attach them to a robot shaped like a very large rodent.

'This is our robot rat. It will eventually be able to feel its way around in the dark by using its whiskers, just like real rats do.'

'And why on earth are you trying to build a robot rat?' asked Nick.

'One reason is to try and understand how real rats navigate. We have a hunch about how rat brains work, but we don't know if it's correct, so we're programming our robot rat to operate in the way we think real rats work. If the robot starts behaving like a real rat, that will mean we're probably on the right track.'

Nick raised his eyebrows. 'Does it have any practical uses?'

'Yes, but it's kind of secret.'

'Military?'

I nodded conspiratorially. 'Let's put it this way; a robot that can find its way around a cave in the dark, without giving itself away by shining a light ahead of it, could come in handy in certain situations.'

'So, Bin Laden is sitting in his cave in Afghanistan, and all of a sudden a robot rat appears. What's the rat going to do? Arrest him? Or will it be a rat suicide bomber?'

'Stranger things have happened. In World War Two the US military hatched a plan to attach little firebombs to bats and drop them by aircraft over Tokyo. The little creatures would fly into the attics of the wooden houses and hang from the rafters and – boom!'

'The US military has always been pretty creative, I guess.'

'And they do fund a hell of a lot of research in robotics,' I said. 'Don't bite the hand that feeds you.'

I showed Nick around the rest of the lab, finishing at my own little area, where my research assistant Peter sat at a desk behind a disembodied head.

'This is Peter,' I said. Then, pointing to the head, 'And this is Eva.'

Eva's face was clearly female. She had large brown eyes, long dark eyelashes and full red lips. Her skin, however, only stretched as far back as her ears and forehead. Behind that, where the hair should have been, was a chaotic arrangement of little motors, which pulled little wires attached to the back of the skin on her face.

By activating the motors in different combinations, we could program Eva to make a variety of facial expressions.

'It's creepy!' exclaimed Nick. 'The skin doesn't look quite right. It's a bit too rubbery.'

'Yeah, skin is one of the hardest things to get right. And it's quite normal to find it creepy. It's the valley of the uncanny.'

'The what?'

'The valley of the uncanny. It's a theory put forward by a Japanese roboticist in the 1970s. He argued that robots would become more acceptable as they came to resemble people more closely, but only up to a point. When the resemblance is almost, but not quite, perfect, people will suddenly experience a kind of revulsion.'

Nick leaned over towards Eva so his eyes were on a level with hers. He seemed to be looking for some kind of reaction, as if he thought there might be a soul lurking behind the blank expression.

Peter hit a button on his keyboard, and Eva sprang to life. She tilted her head back, fluttered her eyelashes a couple of times, and made a big smile.

Nick recoiled in horror. 'Jesus!' he said. 'She made me jump!'

Eva's lips turned down at the sides and she frowned.

'Aaah! Sorry! Poor thing. I didn't mean to offend you,' apologized Nick. 'Damn, it's a bloody robot! What on earth am I saying?'

'You see?' I smiled. 'It's quite easy to start projecting

some kind of personality onto these robots, even if it's just a head on a stand with no hair.'

'Right,' said Nick, recovering his composure. 'Let's do the interview.'

We sat down in my cubicle and I proceeded to explain how I had become increasingly alarmed by the dangers of climate change, peak oil and various other threats facing our modern world. What if they reached some kind of tipping point, and civilization collapsed? How would the survivors cope with life after the crash? This was what I wanted to explore in the course of the Utopia Experiment.

When Nick's book, entitled *How to Live Off-Grid*, came out a year later, I was rather surprised by his description of me. 'Dylan is in his mid-thirties,' he wrote, 'with small delicate features and mousy hair.' So far so good. But then he added:

> Behind rimless glasses, his eyes, I have to admit, were glinting madly, and with his deep, almost expressionless voice and self-effacing mannerisms, he fitted the stereotype of a scientist who believes that humanity must be saved from itself, whatever the cost.

Was Nick exaggerating for effect? Or was I already that far gone?

4. HOSPITAL

In hospital, I was beginning to ask some tentative questions about my real reasons for doing the Utopia Experiment. The blind panic and utter incomprehension that had precipitated my crisis still raged through my mind most of the day, but there were occasional moments when I calmed down for long enough to think slightly more clearly.

In these moments, I began to probe for the first time my ulterior motives for embarking on my bizarre project. From conception in Mexico, through the months of preparation, and right up to those terrible days in May 2007 when the scales fell from my eyes, I never paused to ask myself what psychological forces or personal issues might be propelling me along this strange path. I was completely focused on what I saw as the objective facts, the external, rational justifications. The world was in a terrible mess, not me. Civilization might collapse. The experiment would be a way of finding out how the survivors would cope. My motives were entirely noble – curiosity, adventure, and a desire to raise awareness of the looming threats to the environment and global civilization.

Now, I wasn't so sure. Beneath the veneer of my official story, I could dimly perceive other motives, not quite so admirable. Was I simply seeking a way out of a job that I wasn't qualified for, and had no reasonable prospects of excelling at? My PhD was in philosophy, but I had somehow managed to talk myself into a job in robotics, despite having no background in engineering or AI. I'm a fast learner, but I was soon way out of my depth, and it was becoming clear that while I could probably tread water for another year or two, I would never become an expert in the field or a leading researcher. Was the Utopia Experiment merely a cover story to help me stage a graceful exit from a path that was going nowhere?

Maybe. But why concoct such an *elaborate* cover story? There had to be more to it than that. In the course of my conversations with Dr Satoshi I began to touch on other reasons why I might have become so preoccupied with the collapse of civilization, worries that had nothing to do with the state of the world out there, but were of a more subjective nature.

I recalled a conversation I had had with a veteran of self-sufficiency, a man called Mick, who had lived for many years in a very remote area in the West Highlands. It was late in the evening, a few days after I had arrived in Scotland to start the experiment. Mick and I were sitting at a large kitchen table in Romay's house, each nursing a glass of whisky. Mick was deep in thought, digesting what I had just explained to him about the Utopia Experiment.

'It's a simulation,' I had told him, when he asked what it was all about. 'I've recruited some volunteers via my website, and we're going to act as if we're living in the aftermath of a catastrophic failure of global civilization.'

I explained we were going to live in yurts, since they would keep us warm in the cold winter months. But Mick wasn't worried about the practical details. He was thinking about the hidden motivations and fears he suspected lay behind my rather unusual idea.

'The end of the world, eh?' He took another sip. 'That's always just another way of pondering your own mortality,' he said.

A psychiatric hospital is a blunt instrument for treating mental illness. You take someone whose life has disintegrated and put them in a building with other lunatics. Once or twice a day you give them some medication, and once a week the doctor pays a visit. That's more or less it.

That leaves a lot of time for doing nothing. It's probably necessary to have some time for just resting, for not doing the crazy manic stuff that is likely to make things worse. But since mental illness often involves the loss of any daily routine, it is also important to try to rebuild some kind of structure. The nurses did their best to help me construct a rudimentary timetable, prodding me out of bed in the mornings, and taking me for occasional walks outside the hospital.

One time, a nurse spotted me pacing frantically around the courtyard, and came over to see if she could calm me down.

'Don't worry, Dylan. Things aren't so bad. What's the worst that can happen?'

Perhaps the nurse thought I would conclude that the worst wasn't all that bad after all, and cheer up. But this isn't a good question to ask someone who has spent the past year worrying about the collapse of civilization. It immediately prompted a cascade of rich visual images, culminating in a picture of me suffering a particularly horrible death.

The fictional scenario I had written to set the scene for my experiment in futurology had ended on a positive note, as the survivors returned to a more humane way of life, free from the curse of modern technology. But the past months had unmasked that fantasy, and shown me how bleak life would really be in the aftermath of global collapse. When I looked back on that narrative from my hospital bed, I wondered at how I had conjured some blissful rural idyll out of a post-apocalyptic nightmare. When it came to acting my scenario out in the real world, the transformation was precisely the opposite.

The nurses wouldn't let me ruminate for too long, however; they nagged me into signing up for a variety of activities, from cookery classes and tai-chi to gym sessions and art therapy.

Art therapy turned out to be rather fun. The teacher was a carefree woman who played classical music on her stereo while four or five of us dabbed away at large sheets of paper with watercolours. When she asked me if I would like to choose a CD to put on, I rifled through her collection and picked out one by Vivaldi. I can't remember what was on that CD, because the moment it started playing all I could hear was another piece by Vivaldi that I'm pretty sure wasn't in her library.

> *Sum in medio tempestatum*
> *quasi navis agitata,*
> *conturbata, inter horridas procellas.*
> *Hinc horrores, hinc terrores,*
> *fremunt venti, nescio portum*
> *nec amicas cerno stellas.*

> I am in the midst of a storm,
> like a ship which is tossed about,
> rocked amidst terrible waves.
> Horrors from this side, terrors from that,
> the winds rage, I know of no harbour
> and I cannot see the friendly stars.

As the voice of the soprano soared up and down in my head, I clumsily painted a crude picture of a boat in a storm, a not too subtle metaphor for my troubled soul. And my mind drifted back to that time, a year ago, when I had set out from the Cotswolds, bound for Scotland, my heart bursting with enthusiasm for the adventure that lay ahead of me.

When my mother came to visit me, a few days later, I was at a loss for words. All I could think was to show her the pictures I'd painted. I spread them out on my bed for her to look at. There was something childlike about them, with their crude watercolour images and amateurish brush strokes – the first paintings I had done since high school. A portrait of one my fellow patients. The picture of the boat caught up in Vivaldi's tempest. And an eerie, sad self-portrait with suitably vacant eyes that quite by accident captured my disconnected state of mind.

My mother looked at the pictures stoically, as if this was all perfectly normal, and I did my best to keep up the pretence.

We hugged as she wiped away a tear; I smiled weakly. She had flown up from England at Dr Satoshi's request; it wasn't strictly necessary, but she had been happy to do whatever she could.

'Dr Satoshi has asked me to make some notes for him,' she said. 'Anything I can think of that might throw some light on your condition. Stuff about your childhood. Anything that struck me as unusual about you when you were younger.'

I tried to smile again, but I was too sad. I could picture myself as a small child, running through the long grass in the fields near our house in south-west England, while my mother and my sister strolled along behind me.

My mother could never have imagined then that, almost four decades later, she would be visiting her boy in a psychiatric hospital, looking more helpless and fragile than he did all those years ago, in the Gloucestershire sunshine.

Is that when it started, my madness – if that is what it was? Was the Utopia Experiment merely the first visible shoot to spring from seeds planted long before, waiting patiently for the right moment to germinate and spread their silent roots through the dark soil of my imagination? Were those seeds planted in my childhood, or in my genome, some black inheritance from my father perhaps? Was I born that way? Did I come into the world with a fevered mind? These were the questions that Dr Satoshi wanted my mother to answer, but though she searched her memory for any possible clues, she couldn't find any smoking guns. There was the time, when I was eight, when I had jumped out of a window at our house in Kent because I couldn't bear the sound of my parents arguing. But although the gesture seemed dramatic to them, I had a pretty good idea I wouldn't injure myself. The drop was about ten feet, and there was grass below, so I didn't even get a bruise. It clearly left a lasting impression in my mother's mind, but it didn't provide the key to my mental illness.

The truth was, my mother never realized how gloomy I was when I was a kid. She saw that I often spent time alone, but only because my head would be buried in a book. I myself don't even recall feeling glum in my younger years, and it was only when I looked through my childhood diaries, many years later, that I uncovered the unmistakable traces of persistent sadness that foreshadowed the bouts of depression from which I would begin to suffer in my early thirties.

'So when did you first get depressed?' asked Dr Satoshi.

'It was in the winter of 1996, I think. I was in Buffalo, upstate New York.'

'What were you doing there?'

'I was studying for a PhD,' I said. 'I was really unhappy. It was cold and snowy, and I was really missing my friends in London. But the gloom was deeper and darker than anything I had experienced before, and I began to suffer from horrible panic attacks. Things got a bit better when I left Buffalo and went back to England to do my PhD at the London School of Economics instead. But it returned a year later. That's when I went to see a doctor.'

'And did that help?'

'Yes,' I nodded. 'I was lucky. The antidepressants worked pretty well. I came off the medication after six months, and I was fine again for a couple of years.'

'And then?'

'I had two more episodes of depression in the following years, but they also cleared up quite quickly when I went back on the pills. I was pretty sensible about it. I would head back to the doctor as soon as I spotted the early warning signs.'

'And what were they?'

'The first sign was usually a loss of energy. I would begin to feel much more tired than usual, and I would start sleeping during the day. But then I would wake up very early in the morning, feeling panicky and upset.'

'That's quite typical,' said Dr Satoshi. 'Early morning waking.'

'Then things that previously seemed easy, like going shopping or delivering a lecture, would begin to seem much more difficult and intimidating. And, gradually, life would begin to seem less meaningful. My everyday interests, usually so absorbing, would lose their significance, and everything would seem – well, just pointless.'

'Anything else?'

'Yes. It's strange, but I would begin to notice dirt more often, especially dirty bits of my own house. It was as if the whole world was decaying, and could never be cleaned up, no matter how hard anyone tried. And I would burst into tears for no apparent reason, suddenly and unexpectedly, at random moments during the day.'

'Did you ever have suicidal thoughts?'

'Not until the past couple of months,' I said. 'In all my previous episodes I never made any plans to kill myself, but I did wish I was dead. I would sit around and long for an early death.'

'And did you experience these same thoughts and feelings in Utopia?'

'Yes,' I said, 'all of them.'

'So why didn't you go back to the doctor right away, as you did before?'

'I don't know.' I scratched my head. 'Maybe I wanted to be true to the scenario we were acting out in the experiment. There wouldn't be any doctors or antidepressants after civilization collapsed. And maybe it was because I thought depression was just a symptom of modern civilization, and it would go away naturally if I was living in a natural environment.'

'But it didn't.'

'No, it got worse and worse. I slid further down the slope than ever before. And by the time I did go to see a doctor, I was in a terrible state.'

'Yes,' nodded Dr Satoshi, 'you certainly were.'

My mother had bought me a few books to read in hospital. One of them was *The God Delusion* by Richard Dawkins. The title captures the idea that believing in God is as mistaken and bizarre as thinking that you are the emperor of China or that aliens have removed your brain. But when I caught a few of the nurses eyeing the book suspiciously, I realized it could be interpreted another way. Did they think it was about people who believed that they were gods? Did they think I was one of those people? But maybe there was something to the idea. A week before I left for Scotland, I had an argument with my friend Caroline on the phone. She had tried to warn me that I was taking on too much, but I dismissed all her qualms with arrogant complacency.

Then she asked me what I hoped to achieve by doing the experiment.

'I want to inspire people!' I said.

'What makes you think people need inspiring?' she asked.

'Most people lead such shallow, drab, hopeless lives. They are craving for something more, some sense of adventure. I want to show them they don't have to settle for bourgeois mediocrity. They can do greater things!'

'What, like giving up your job and living in a field in Scotland?'

'They might realize civilization is going to the dogs,' I said. 'They might start living in a more sustainable way. They might even come and join me!'

Caroline went quiet for a bit. Then she breathed a sigh of exasperation.

'Listen to yourself, Dylan!' she said. 'You've got a fucking god complex!'

5. ADAM

As the spring of 2006 turned into summer, and the time to leave for Scotland drew nearer, I was becoming more of a committed doomer. I was devouring books by new doomsayers with impeccable scientific credentials. In *Our Final Century* (2003), Martin Rees argued that humanity only had a 50 per cent chance of surviving to the year 2100 – and he was the Astronomer Royal, no less! In *The Revenge of Gaia* (2006), the renowned ecologist James Lovelock painted a terrifying vision of a 'hot arid world' in which a few survivors 'gather for the journey to the new Arctic centres of civilization'. In *Collapse* (2005), Jared Diamond described how many former civilizations had committed 'ecocide'.

It was at this point I sketched out the fictional scenario that would set the scene for the experiment, and posted it online. I drew heavily on the work of Thomas Homer-Dixon, a Canadian political scientist who argued that 'tectonic stresses' were accumulating deep underneath the surface of the global order. The increasing scarcity of conventional oil was just one piece of the puzzle. There was also growing economic instability, increasing environmental damage, and climate change. Together, all these stresses were combining to create a perfect storm.

I was so keenly aware of the omens that presaged global disaster that I entirely missed the warning signs of my own personal one. I completely failed to spot the ambiguity in the title of an article I wrote for the *Guardian* in December 2005: 'A risk of total collapse'. I watched *Donnie Darko*, and ignored the obvious psychological interpretation; to me, Frank wasn't a figment of Donnie's diseased imagination, but a real giant rabbit, with genuine information about the end of the world.

The experiment was now becoming, in my mind, more than just a simulation, a way of imagining what life after a crash *might* be like; it was becoming a preparation for the real thing. The more I contemplated the idea of global collapse, the more it became not just a possibility, but a near certainty. Whereas at first I had been surprised if anyone took my worries seriously, I was now amazed if they didn't.

I remember picking up the phone one evening and calling my sister to tell her about my plans.

'Hey, Charlotte, I've got a great idea!'

Charlotte had heard me say that many times before. 'What now?'

I recognized the slightly tentative note in her voice.

She's always been sceptical and sensible, but I couldn't imagine her not getting excited about this.

'I'm going to set up an experiment.'

'OK. What kind of experiment?'

'An experiment in post-apocalyptic living.'

There was silence on the other end of the phone.

I was amazed by her failure to grasp the importance of the project, and worried that she would be stranded in London when the crash came. I remember urging her to buy a horse so that she would have some means of transport when the oil ran out. If only she could find a paddock near her flat in Notting Hill, to keep the horse in, she might be able to ride up to Scotland to join me and my fellow survivalists, and so escape the nightmarish last days of London, as the city imploded in a frenzy of looting and disease. None of this seemed odd to me at the time, and I was puzzled by the fact that Charlotte seemed to find it so.

On the other hand, my fictional scenario struck a chord with many of the people who wrote to me to volunteer. Even David Ross, the no-nonsense former Royal Marine, emailed me enthusiastically to say that he shared my views about the likelihood of global collapse. He was skilled in making boots and rucksacks, and offered to clothe and shoe the community. He also admitted to being handy with a chainsaw and a scythe.

David would turn out to be one of the most practical and helpful of all the volunteers. In fact, with four or five Davids, things might have turned out very differently.

But that wasn't the point. I wanted to see how a random bunch of survivors from a modern high-tech society would cope when there was no more electricity, no more oil and no more government. A bunch of former marines would have been cheating.

In April and May, as I made my final preparations, I visited a number of eco-villages and alternative communities to learn about living off-grid. My first port of call was Coed Hills in South Wales.

Coed (pronounced *coyd*, from the Welsh word for woods) was set on the top of a hill amid the lush greenery of the Vale of Glamorgan, not far from Cardiff. When I arrived, slanting rays of evening sunshine bathed the strange assortment of buildings – railway carriages, Mongolian yurts, log cabins, teepees and straw-bale huts – in a warm golden light. I parked my car and wandered into what looked like the main building, an old stone barn that had been converted into a large living area and meeting space.

Inside, a motley crew was preparing supper. Dressed in a strange assortment of woolly hats, old jumpers, puffa jackets, combat trousers and muddy boots, they shuffled around the stove without even a glance towards the newcomer. All I had to go on was a name that my friend Angus had given me.

'Is Rawley here?' I asked.

'No, he's away,' replied a tall guy with ginger dread-locks and a bushy beard.

Rawley Clay was the great-grandson of Scouts founder Lord Baden-Powell. Coed Hills was his brain-child, and the land had belonged to his father. Angus had told me to look for a man in a felt suit surrounded by lots of dogs or reciting poetry in a large homemade birdcage. I was very disappointed he wasn't at home.

Eventually one of the residents took pity on the stranger in their midst, and offered to show me round before the sun went down. I nodded eagerly, and we headed off while the others put the final touches to supper.

We walked past the permaculture gardens, where a variety of vegetables and herbs grew in raised beds, and along a trail dotted with rustic sculptures, into the woods, where a sawmill and green woodworking area emerged from a carpet of fresh sawdust. Further into the woods, more benders and homemade yurts nestled among the trees, with faint wisps of smoke winding out of aluminium stovepipes.

Making our way back to the buildings, we passed a row of compost toilets, a couple of goats, and a mys-terious building that seemed to contain a pile of large batteries.

'Storing energy is the hardest bit,' said Richard. 'Generating it is easy, but to store it we still need to rely on dirty old batteries.' The whole site was run on alterna-tive energy, he explained, from a high-tech wind turbine and a large solar panel that tracked the sun like a flower, to biomass underfloor heaters and solar showers made out of scrap radiators.

This was all new to me, and I was taking copious mental notes as Richard explained how the various systems worked. If civilization collapsed, I thought, this is the kind of place where I would want to be. It was pretty much self-sufficient in terms of energy, food and building materials. And it managed to achieve this with a kind of elegance, ingenuity and simplicity that was aesthetically appealing too. I felt inspired.

A week later, I received an email from a man called Adam. He said he had heard about my experiment from some people at Coed Hills, and was drawn to my vision of a perfect community.

I was intrigued, and invited Adam to visit the lab a few days later. I guessed from the email that he was a bit eccentric, but nothing prepared me for the ragged traveller I saw when I greeted him at the reception desk. In his early fifties, he was dressed in a British Airways blanket and a cowboy hat, with a feather poking out of the hatband. His grey beard and gnarled face made me think of Gandalf from *Lord of the Rings*, but his soft blue eyes and friendly smile made him seem much more approachable than that intimidating wizard.

I could only imagine what my colleagues thought of me as I showed this eccentric figure briefly round the lab, before whisking him off to my cubicle, out of sight. I felt slightly guilty about my embarrassment, though. After all, wasn't I determined to break away from the conventions of society, to leave this respectable existence behind? I saw Adam as a sign of the new life that awaited me in Scotland, one in which we would no doubt all have to dress in whatever clothes we could find or make ourselves. Perhaps I would come to look as strange as he did.

I would later learn that Adam was not his real name (or at least, 'not the name the humans gave me', as he put it), but one he had given himself when he 'left the world of man' in 2004. Before then he had lived a fairly normal life, but after he received his 'call' he set out on the road as a 'spiritual pilgrim'. He gave away everything he had except for a few hundred pounds. Within three weeks, all the money was gone, and Adam was homeless. Now he wandered the country from one community to another, seeking to promote his strange gospel, which was a mishmash of New Age ideas and an idiosyncratic interpretation of Christianity that seemed to draw heavily on Dan Brown.

But at that first meeting, Adam told me none of this. He confined himself to making practical suggestions for my experiment, in what I later suspected was a deliberate attempt to hide his wacky beliefs.

'Why don't you build some yurts!' he urged, his eyes gleaming.

'Sure,' I said. 'Can you teach me how?'

'I'll do better than that!' exclaimed Adam. 'I'll start

building a couple of yurts now. I'm heading off to another community next week in Hereford. They have plenty of wood there, and some canvas, and a sewing machine. If you come out and visit me there next month, you can see for yourself.'

So a few weeks later I drove out to Hereford. Eco-villages, yurt camps and other kinds of alternative community vary widely in their visibility to the outside world and openness to visitors. Coed Hills had official opening hours, ran courses in sustainable living, and had a beautiful website. The place I visited in Hereford was at the other end of the spectrum. It had no planning permission. Nobody except the residents and a few travellers knew it was there. It didn't even have a name.

Adam had given me directions to the camp, which was tucked away in a wood on a private estate near the Welsh border. I turned into the estate and drove on an unmarked road with oak trees and pastures on either side. After about a mile the road became a dirt track and entered a thick forest. Then, to the left, I saw an opening with a campfire and a few yurts. I parked my car and Adam came to greet me as I got out. He briefly introduced me to a ragged bunch sitting around the fire, before leading me over to another clearing and proudly pointing out the two new yurts he had made for Utopia. They did look rather impressive. The blue canvas coverings had been expertly stitched together on an old-fashioned Singer sewing machine. Bending down to roll up the flap covering the doorway, Adam ushered me inside.

'This is your yurt,' he said.

A couple of candles were burning, casting a flickering light on the lattice of hazel poles – still with the bark on – that formed the yurt's skeleton. I spread out my sleeping bag on the floor and lay down on top of it. This would be the first night that I had ever slept in a yurt, but I already felt at home. The rustic, circular structure seemed to emanate a calming influence, stilling the mind and slowing the pulse.

Adam broke my reverie by thrusting his head through the doorway to tell me supper was ready. Back at the campfire a waif-like girl with long tawny dreadlocks was dishing out bowls of bean stew from a steaming cauldron, while her two-year-old son ran naked around the dusty clearing. Her name was Shakti, she said, and she was from the Rainbow People, who were here on a scouting mission to find a suitable spot for the next international Rainbow Gathering. As we sat around the fire eating supper, I learned that this place was very different from Coed. There were no vegetable gardens here; people bought what they needed in the local town, using the meagre proceeds they raised by busking and begging. Nor did they generate their own electricity. Their camp was, in fact, entirely parasitic on the civilization they rejected, and if that civilization collapsed, the inhabitants would not survive any longer than those leading more comfortable lives in the towns and cities. It was, in essence, no more than a refuge for hippies and dropouts. But in one sense it was still very like Coed: here, as there, the land belonged to the founder's father, who had allowed his son to indulge his alternative lifestyle, and the other inhabitants were mostly hangers-on.

'I can do better than this!' I thought to myself. I might not be able to put together something as impressive as Coed Hills in the eighteen months I had given myself, but those of us at Utopia could surely grow our own food. We certainly wouldn't be popping down to the supermarket every week! And we would have a vision, a mission even. We would be exploring an apocalyptic scenario, which would endow our every action with meaning and send a warning to the whole world about the dangers of climate change and peak oil. There was no shared value system in this ragtag community beyond a vague antipathy to work, I scoffed.

After supper, I made my way back to the yurt Adam had built for me. It was a warm and dry spring evening, but as I slid into my sleeping bag I thought the yurt would be sturdy enough to withstand a strong Highland wind. Yurts are perfectly suited for the harsh Mongolian climate. A stove in the middle is fed continually with yak dung to keep it burning day and night, while thick layers of felt trap the warmth inside and make it nice and snug. That, I thought, would be vital in the Scottish winter.

But, as I would be reminded frequently over the ensuing months, Scotland is not just cold. It is also wet – much wetter, in fact, than Mongolia. And though our yurts had an extra layer of rough homemade canvas on top of the felt, this was not enough to keep out the kind of persistent, unrelenting rainfall that makes Scotland such a wonderful place to live.

A considerable amount of our time in the Utopia Experiment would, therefore, be spent trying to keep the rain out of our yurts. This did not make for particularly pleasant sleeping conditions. Often I would drowse off warm and dry, the stove burning (with wood, not yak dung) and the canvas firmly tied down, only to awake in the dead of night, bitterly cold, to find the stove had gone out and the rain was dripping through gaps in the canvas that had been fumbled open by the wind. I would lie shivering in my sleeping bag, unwilling to get out and tie the canvas back down for fear of getting even colder and wetter, cursing Adam and his *fucking* yurts.

The eco-villages of today, and the hippy communes of the sixties, are just the latest in a long line of utopian experiments, stretching back thousands of years. The first Christian monasteries were established in Egypt in the fourth century CE, and the first Buddhist monasteries some five centuries earlier. Plymouth Colony and Pennsylvania were different kinds of religious utopias, as were the Jesuit Reductions in Paraguay. Socialist utopias, such as Robert Owen's New Harmony in Indiana and John Vandeleur's Ralahine in Ireland, began to spring up in the nineteenth century.

What is remarkable about all these diverse experiments is how much they have in common. A relatively small group of people – rarely more than two or three hundred, and often a lot fewer – live and work together, with at least some property held in common, and a relatively non-hierarchical, communal system of decision-making. There is often an emphasis on simple living and self-sufficiency, which usually includes growing much of one's own food. There is also typically an explicit ideology that justifies these practices, though the nature of this belief system can vary widely, which suggests that it is the practices that come first. It's as if there is a perennial urge to return to a simpler way of life that manifests itself in similar ways at different times and places. When this urge overtakes them, people justify their behaviour in terms of the ideas available to them at the time.

Some of these experiments last for decades, but most seem to fall apart within a few years. Brook Farm, one of the most famous utopian communities of the nineteenth century, was typical in this and many other respects. Founded by the social reformer George Ripley in 1841, the little commune in West Roxbury, Massachusetts, was already in decline after just three years. When the writer and preacher Orestes Brownson visited in October 1844, he wrote that 'the atmosphere of the place is horrible'. Financial difficulties meant that the residents had to go without meat, coffee, tea and butter, and the following year an outbreak of smallpox infected twenty-six Brook Farmers, though no one died. When an ambitious communal building known as the Phalanstery, intended to house 'a large and commodious kitchen, a dining-hall capable of seating from three to four hundred persons, two public saloons, and a spacious hall or lecture room', burned down in 1846, the residents began drifting away. One of them recalled the closing months of Brook Farm in later life, observing that they 'seemed dreamy and unreal'.

> It was like a knotted skein slowly unraveling. It was as the ice becomes water, and runs silently away . . . It was like apple blossoms dropping from the trees . . . It was like a thousand and one changing and fading things in nature.

Such would be my experience when my own utopian experiment began to fall apart, less than a year after I had started it. The last few months still seem dreamy and unreal to me too. But I do not look back on them fondly, as John Codman did when he wrote those mournful words about the end of Brook Farm.

Why do these experiments usually fail, and fail so quickly? Why do utopias so often turn into dystopias?

I suspect it may be something to do with the very idea of wiping the slate clean, of resetting the clock to year zero, and building anew from scratch. For while the institutions that the idealists wish to replace are often riddled with flaws, they also embody the accumulated wisdom of many generations, of hundreds of years of R & D. Their bugs may be easier to spot than their features. And perhaps some of the flaws are not mere accidents of history, but inherent in any kind of social organization. People form groups because they have overlapping interests, but the overlap is always partial, and conflicts will always arise at the zones where they fail to coincide.

The rapid failure of these experiments may also be due to the kind of people they attract. Idealists are seldom very practical people. They have impossibly high expectations, and when reality does not live up to them, disillusionment sets in. And when they disagree about how the perfect society should be organized, as they inevitably will, their quarrels will be more bitter, because they care so much more. Utopias also attract misfits, whose inability to integrate may not be due to the society they blame, but to their own cantankerous personalities.

Scale also plays a part. Small communities are like pressure cookers, with no relief valve. Tensions are exacerbated when you rub shoulders with the same few people all day every day, absent the balm of consanguinity to soothe the irritation. It is one thing to live in a large extended family group, as our ancestors did before they started farming, and quite another to spend all your time with a bunch of strangers, with little opportunity to escape from those you dislike. Jealousy and resentment find fertile soil in such confined spaces. Those who live in towns and cities may yearn for the intimacy of village life, but if they were to find themselves transported to some rural hamlet, most would soon long for the anonymity of urban existence.

I certainly failed to anticipate the extent to which the volunteers would end up getting on my nerves. 'Evans,' wrote one journalist who interviewed me about the project a month before I headed to Scotland, 'has an extremely rosy view of how the community will sort out disagreements.' She was right: I pictured a harmonious group of fellow survivors, all glowing with affection for one another, like the beautiful young things the protagonist finds when he first arrives on the island in *The Beach*. I had conveniently forgotten the later scenes, when a wounded member of the community is taken out into the jungle and left to die, so his cries of pain won't interfere with the merry-making. Or when the leader is prepared to kill to preserve the community's isolation. For someone who claimed to know so much about the theory of human nature, I sure didn't seem to understand it very well in practice.

The few utopian communities that survive more than a decade are mostly religious in nature. Some monasteries have lasted for hundreds of years, and many Amish communities in the United States still keep the customs their ancestors brought with them when they migrated from Europe over two hundred years ago. But I'm an atheist, and I wanted my experiment to be free from any whiff of dogma. On my website, for example, I had stated that one aim of the project was 'to see how a community can form around emergent values, values that emerge from the interactions of group members, rather than being adopted lock, stock and barrel from a religion or a political creed'.

The word *emergent* harked back to my research in robotics. In the swarm intelligence paradigm, lots of very stupid robots are programmed to work together in such a way that a kind of collective intelligence emerges from their interactions. When I began laying out the aims of the project, I assumed that people would be almost as easy to experiment with as robots. I would have laughed off such a suggestion, of course, if you had put it to me back then. But I now think that word *emergent* revealed a rather naive – and perhaps even callous – belief that I could simply put a bunch of humans together in the Scottish wilderness in the same way that I put a bunch of robots together in the lab. I could set up the initial conditions, flick a switch, and watch what happened. And what would happen would be some kind of marvellous coordination, as a new set of values – non-religious values, of course – simply emerged from their interactions. In viewing my volunteers as somewhat akin to robots in the lab, I overlooked not just the greater complexity of human beings, but also my own previous doubts about human coordination. After all, hadn't I contrasted human societies *unfavourably* with robot ones? Back in the lab, it had always struck me that while a bunch of stupid robots could behave intelligently as a group, otherwise intelligent people seemed to behave like idiots whenever you put them together.

I was also naively egalitarian in my thinking. In

swarm robotics, all the robots are exactly the same. There is no leader. And in my experiment there would be no leader either, no authoritarian figure to impose values from on high. The values would just *emerge* – right? – from interactions between equal individuals. But of course that was to overlook the peculiar nature of my own role in the experiment. I was to be simultaneously the founder and just another one of the volunteers. I wanted to join in the daily work with everyone else, to participate while I observed, and let things take their own course. But at the same time, it would be me who set the parameters. I had conceived of the whole idea in the first place and written the basic scenario that would govern our narrative. It was my experiment, after all.

I would later find this dual role increasingly hard to manage as the experiment progressed. In trying to be simultaneously participant and organizer, I would end up being neither. It would prove to be one of many contradictions pulling me in opposite directions, causing me to oscillate at ever greater frequencies, until finally everything flew apart. Like Nick Carraway, the narrator of *The Great Gatsby*, I would be 'within and without', unable to immerse myself completely in the daily activities because I would be fretting about logistics, and unable to plan properly because I would be called over to help carry some wood or chase after an escaped pig.

Of course I would inevitably play some kind of leading role. But I didn't want to be a charismatic figure, let alone a dictator. I wanted to blend into the background, and watch what happened.

Or did I? Was there perhaps some secret desire to be a kind of guru or cult leader, some unacknowledged form of megalomania?

6. SCOTLAND

I didn't really have to sell my house to fund the experiment. I could have rented it out and moved back in after my sojourn in Scotland was over. With less money to blow on ill thought-out acquisitions that quickly fell into disuse – like the pathetic little solar panel that only generated enough electricity to power a single light bulb for a couple of hours a day – I could probably have done the experiment for a fraction of what I eventually spent.

Nor did I have to give up my job. If I'd asked for a sabbatical, or taken unpaid leave, I would have had a job to go back to when the experiment was over. But deep down, there was a part of me that wanted to dispense with any safety nets, and cut off any possible avenue of retreat. So it wasn't enough even to quit my job; I had to make a big show of condemning the whole academic system, which would make it hard to get another job in any university in the UK. In an interview for the *Times Higher Education Supplement* in April 2006, I complained that there was 'a ridiculous amount of bureaucracy and frustration' at most universities. 'People don't have excited looks on their faces anymore.'

All of the interesting, creative people who really inspired me were getting old, I said, and there didn't seem to be any younger people in academia with the potential to take their place. 'As you look further down the age spectrum, you get less and less evidence of thinking outside the box and being zany,' I moaned. 'It's not because they are any less intelligent, it's just that it's all dictated from above. There's no real time for academics to do the creative brooding.' I decried 'the lack of autonomy and everything pinned on learning outcomes. I don't know why academics feel the need to ape this audit culture that has come into universities from the business world.' There was a real mood of pessimism, I pontificated, without the slightest suspicion that I might be projecting my own feelings onto the rest of my colleagues.

My heroes, I went on, tended to be on the margins of academia, like the philosopher George Santayana. 'His creativity went up dramatically when he left academia,' I said; 'I would love to be like that.'

As another journalist noted when she interviewed me for *The Times* at around the same time, there was 'a strong whiff of burnt bridges'. And I could see that too, even then. I was setting fire to those bridges deliberately, driven by a mixture of excitement for my project, and scorn for the life I was leaving behind.

My friend Caroline said she would miss visiting me in my Cotswold cottage, and I invited her to come over for one last weekend to say goodbye. She asked if she could bring a friend with her, and the two of them arrived one sunny Saturday afternoon in May.

Caroline's friend was called Bo. She was in her thirties, and tall, with shoulder-length straight hair dyed blonde. I had met her once before, several years previously, apparently, though I could barely remember it.

I felt instantly attracted to Bo, and over the next few weeks I visited her in London several times. As we grew closer, we began to wonder what would happen to our relationship when I left for Scotland. This was not something I had anticipated. I had broken up with my previous girlfriend just before going to Mexico, and I had always imagined myself doing the Utopia Experiment as a single man, without the encumbrance of a partner to care for. Now, however, the idea began to form in my mind of inviting Bo to come with me. So what if she had kids? Maybe her son, who was ten, would stay in London with his father, and Bo would just bring her six-year-old daughter with her to Scotland.

I had visions of the three of us living together in a yurt like some rustic Mongolian family. Instead of a single man at the heart of the experiment, there would be a couple with a small child, a microcosm of the new society that would emerge from the ashes of the old.

When my last day at work came, my colleagues held an informal meeting to say goodbye and wish me luck with my new venture. I had only discussed my plans with one or two of them, but word had spread, and some had no doubt read the interviews in the newspapers in which I damned academic life and scorned the lack of creativity in my peers. They were remarkably forgiving of my haughtiness; one of them even baked a cake.

We gathered in a nondescript meeting room in the engineering building at 11 am and Janice, the head of department, made a few remarks.

'We'll be sad to see you go,' she said, in a kind-hearted tone of voice. 'You've certainly livened the place up.'

There were a few smiles as someone passed round coffee and cake.

'We clubbed together and bought you this as a going-away present,' said Janice, and held up a thick warm fleece. 'We figured you'd need it up there when the winter sets in.'

Everyone chuckled, but not in a mean way. They seemed more concerned and puzzled than scornful. But I scoffed at their doubts and, to show them I was both aware of the difficulties that lay ahead, and determined to overcome them, I read out a short extract from *The Blithedale Romance*. Nathaniel Hawthorne's novel was inspired by his experiences at Brook Farm, where he lived for seven months in 1841. The short extract I read out contrasted his expectations of rural bliss with the dreary reality of life in the community:

While our enterprise lay all in theory, we had pleased

ourselves with delectable visions of the spiritualiza-
tion of labor. It was to be our form of prayer and
ceremonial of worship. Each stroke of the hoe was to
uncover some aromatic root of wisdom, heretofore
hidden from the sun. Pausing in the field, to let the
wind exhale the moisture from our foreheads, we
were to look upward, and catch glimpses into the
far-off soul of truth. In this point of view, matters
did not turn out quite so well as we anticipated. It is
very true that, sometimes, gazing casually around
me, out of the midst of my toil, I used to discern a
richer picturesqueness in the visible scene of earth
and sky ... But this was all. The clods of earth, which
we so constantly belabored and turned over and over,
were never etherealized into thought. Our thoughts,
on the contrary, were fast becoming cloddish. Our
labor symbolized nothing, and left us mentally slug-
gish in the dusk of the evening. Intellectual activity
is incompatible with any large amount of bodily
exercise.

I, of course, was far too knowing to fall prey to the
same disillusionment. I would show my colleagues how
unfounded their concerns were. I was prepared for the
hard times ahead. Indeed, I was looking forward to
them. They would strengthen my body and enrich my
mind. My thoughts would not become cloddish. I would
succeed where Hawthorne had failed.

*

By July, I was finally ready to embark on my journey. My house was sold. I'd quit my job. Most of my worldly possessions had been sent up to Scotland and were now piled high in an old shipping container that sat in a muddy field next to what would soon become Utopia.

Only a few of my most precious things remained, and they easily fitted in my car. Some documents, a laptop and, of course, my cat – Socrates. Like most cats, Socrates was not particularly fond of cars, and I had decided that it would greatly assist him in enduring the long drive if he could chew on a Valium. My vet had even given me a bottle of pills for the purpose – marked *animal Valium*, perhaps to deter me from stealing a few for myself.

After an hour or so of driving, I stopped to check on Socrates. I gently prised open the lid on the cat-box, which was wedged in between some clothes and a suitcase on the back seat, only to see a wide-eyed cat staring back at me with a mixture of anxiety and recrimination. Clearly, one Valium was not enough for this robust feline, so I gave the trusting animal another pill, and continued on my way.

An hour later, I stopped again. Socrates was still wide awake, and looked pissed off with his continuing confinement. Even so, I wasn't sure whether it would be wise to give him a third Valium. I wanted to help him sleep, not kill him. But the thought of the poor beast having to put up with eight or nine more hours in this small cage overcame my qualms, and I gave him a third pill.

When I stopped for lunch, and checked on Socrates again, he was out cold. A little *too* cold, in fact, for my liking. Panicking, I began to prod him, in the hope of triggering some sign of life. Nothing.

'Shit,' I thought. 'I've killed my cat.'

But Socrates wasn't dead. He survived the journey in relatively good form, though he was rather confused when we finally arrived to find no sign of his former abode. When I pitched my little tent down by the river and brought him inside, he sniffed haughtily at the canvas walls before making a dash for the door. If the category 'home' existed in his feline ontology, this was clearly not an example.

What a miserable reward for five years of loyal service! In my old stone cottage Socrates had lived a life of quiet luxury. He would be waiting for me at the front door when I got back from work each day, and lie stretched out like a dog by the fireplace in the long winter evenings, his black fur so hot you could barely touch it. At night he would sleep on my bed by my feet, and climb out of the roof window onto the old stone tiles whenever he fancied a spot of hunting. To go from that to a windy tent in the Scottish Highlands must have come as a terrible blow.

I'm not sure he ever forgave me. Even when we put the yurts up, and installed old cast-iron stoves inside them, he rarely came to visit. Instead, he would hang around the potato shed that became our kitchen and dining room, which at least had stone walls and felt a bit more like a house. Or he would vanish for several days at a time, perhaps to seek refuge in a farmer's house a few miles away, only to reappear with the same look of reproach on his face, as if to say, 'Why, oh why, did you ever take me away from my lovely old house in the Cotswolds, and bring me to this god-forsaken place?'

When I got up that first morning and emerged from my tent, blinking in the early sunshine, I felt a sudden rush of joy. As I stood and looked around me at the little clearing by the river, I could picture a glorious future lying ahead of me in Scotland. Soon there would be two yurts here, and a campfire, with rustic wooden benches arranged round it. In the evenings we would gather here to eat our supper as the fire blazed and some pot bubbled away. We would swap stories about the day's work, and then raise our minds to higher things, no matter what Hawthorne said. We would integrate our daily experiences into the collective story we were telling about life after the apocalypse, and picture ourselves as hardy but happy survivors.

More yurts would eventually spring up, and woodpiles, and rows of vegetables, and fencing to cordon off an area for the pigs. Our bodies would grow strong from the physical labour and our minds refreshed by the natural surroundings, far away from the cities we'd left behind. Maybe there would even be some children running around, playing happily amidst the bracken and the trees.

And at the centre of it all, unassuming but indisputably wise, would be me, the founder, loved and revered by my fellow utopians. My yurt would be bedecked with homemade woollen carpets and fleece blankets. And perhaps Bo would be there too, sharing the yurt with me, the two of us a source of inspiration to the rest of the group, the original couple, a symbol of the love and harmony that would pervade the whole community.

I gathered some sticks and made a small fire by the river. I had brought some basic provisions to keep me going for the first few days, and I treated myself to a breakfast of bacon and eggs. Then I set about clearing a place for the yurts. It was warm and sunny, and scything the bracken and nettles was tiring, but once the area was clear, I started work on a wooden platform for the first yurt. The pieces for the two yurts Adam had made in Hereford were already stacked up in the potato shed, having been brought up by a friend in the back of his van a week before. Adam was due to arrive the following week, and I wanted everything to be ready for us to put up the yurts as soon as he got here. I had no idea how to assemble the bundles of sticks that would soon become our homes.

It took a week of hard work, and the help of a local builder called Keith, to finish the platforms, and when they were done I took a day off to go salmon fishing. It was the last day of the season, and some friends of Romay had invited me to join them early one morning on the Moray Firth. When I arrived at 6 am they were already out on the water, two in a rowing boat, and two others perched on a cairn (a pile of rocks) in the water, holding the other end of the net. Romay's friend George had kindly left a pair of waders for me in the boot of his car, so I slipped them on and waded out to the cairn – well, part of the way, as it got a bit too deep, so George had to row over and take me the rest of the way in the boat.

This kind of fishing is called net sweeping, and it involves standing around in the water for long periods of time looking for any trace of fish. You can spot them by the way the surface of the water changes colour or texture. When you catch sight of the fish, the people in the boat row back in a semi-circle to drag the net around them. And then everyone on the cairn hauls in the net.

In over four hours of fishing we caught three grilse. Grilse are the first salmon of any generation of smolts to return as adults, having spent one winter at sea, growing from a few ounces to small adults of several pounds' weight. Three might not seem like much, but apparently it wasn't such a bad catch. Some days, George told me, they would return home with nothing. It wasn't like this a decade ago, he said, when the waters were full of fish. But now a combination of over-fishing and the growing seal population (which had exploded since the seals had been declared a protected species a few years before) had reduced the fish stocks to very low levels.

George suggested that he might be able to take a few volunteers from the Utopia Experiment out fishing with him next summer. I thought that sounded great, and hoped there would still be some fish left to catch when the time came.

Adam arrived the following day. When I met him at the bus station in Inverness, he was wearing a brown felt trilby with a feather stuck in the hatband, a sleeveless, fur-trimmed sheepskin jacket and black leather shorts worn over long red cycling pants. His bizarre apparel and flamboyant gestures drew puzzled stares from the other passengers milling around him. I ushered him into my car as quickly as possible and sped back to Utopia. I could almost see the rumours spreading among the citizens of the Highlands, whisperings about a weird stranger in their midst, soon to be followed by other misfits, all bound for a shady settlement founded by an eccentric Englishman.

Adam was impressed by the two platforms I had made, and said we could start putting the yurts up right away. We spent the next few hours gradually coaxing the lattices of hazel sticks into place and binding them together with nylon cords, before covering the structure with the blue canvas that Adam had stitched together so expertly. The whole process took a lot longer than I had anticipated, and by late afternoon we had only managed to put up one of the yurts. Even then it still needed a few adjustments so that it would fit snugly on the platform

I had built, which was slightly smaller than it should've been.

After sleeping in a small tent for the past week, the yurts would be sheer luxury, I thought. I could even stand up when I was right in the middle. But rather than sharing the yurt with Adam, I decided to let him have it to himself for his first night in Utopia.

Adam was grateful for this gesture, but insisted that this was not 'his' yurt. Although it would be the place where he slept, he said he didn't feel a strong sense of ownership. If other people wanted to use it, or sleep there, that was fine by him. But, as I would discover many times during the course of the experiment, Adam's noble words were not necessarily in keeping with reality. An hour later, when I crawled into the yurt to have another look, I noticed something odd to one side of his sleeping bag. An incongruous collection of coins, candles, animal bones and discoloured photographs had been carefully arranged on a piece of driftwood. This, Adam informed me, was his shrine. But it was also evidently a marker of territory.

The fluid approach to ownership and usage that Adam espoused was something I hoped might develop over the course of the experiment. It was, I imagined, probably closer to the way our hunter-gatherer ancestors thought. But I wondered if this would be hard when most of us come from a society that encourages people to make sharp distinctions between 'mine' and 'yours' from early childhood.

That evening, we celebrated Adam's arrival and the completion of the first yurt with a delicious stew of beans and tomatoes that we cooked over an open fire. The sun doesn't set until very late in the Highlands in summertime, but by the time we finally went to bed it was quite dark, and I had to find my way back to my little tent with the aid of a torch. I wondered how I would manage when all the batteries had run out, and all the torches were broken, as would be bound to happen sooner or later after civilization collapsed. Would I carry around a flaming stick, like a Viking, or would my eyes become better at seeing in the dark? Or would I simply stay inside my yurt and temporarily relinquish control of Utopia to the creatures of the night?

As I snuggled into my sleeping bag, I thought I heard a wolf howl in the distance. I sat upright and strained my ears, but all I could hear was the faint rustling of the leaves in the breeze. There had been calls for the reintroduction of wolves to the Scottish Highlands in order to deal with the expanding population of red deer, but the sheep farmers strongly objected. I listened a while longer, then decided it had been a figment of my imagination, and lay down again to sleep.

But then I heard it again, clearer this time, and louder – the distinctive sound of a wolf howling. Suddenly, I was afraid. The idea of wild animals prowling around outside my tent as I slept was not particularly appealing, and I began to wish I was nearer to the campfire, which was probably still smouldering. I decided to gather up my sleeping bag and move back to the fire, where we had just eaten supper.

As I emerged from my tent, though, the true source of the sound became apparent. The clouds had dissipated, and in the dim moonlight, that now cast an eerie glow over the clearing in the trees, I could just about make out the silhouette of a man. From the shape of the hat, I recognized Adam, standing upright by the river, his head tilted backwards, as he let out another long, blood-curdling howl.

7. AGRIC

The Scottish Highlands have long been a place of refuge for dropouts, refuseniks, and hippies. The Utopia Experiment was far from the only alternative community, even in our little corner of north-east Scotland, and I was curious to visit some of our kindred spirits. I was especially keen to visit Goshem, set up by Neil Oram in the late 1960s.

I had only come across Neil a month before moving to Scotland, at a music festival near Yeovil, where I heard him give a bizarre talk in a teepee to a small audience of languid hippies. When I later told some of my fellow festival-goers that I had just heard him talk, their eyes widened. 'Wow!' they chorused, in slightly awed tones, 'Neil's been on the scene for years, man.'

Curious to find out more, I recounted this story several times during my first weeks in the Highlands. The reactions here were rather different: some people were slightly suspicious, others were downright hostile. None of this made sense to me; Neil had come across as an eccentric but harmless chap when I had heard him talk at the festival. And when I emailed him to ask if I could visit his little community, his reply had been positively friendly. When I tried to probe a little more deeply as to what made everyone so wary, some muttered darkly about a self-styled guru who presided over a cult in the hills above Loch Ness, but I found this gossip hard to believe.

Nevertheless, I confess I did feel slightly nervous when I set out to visit Goshem with Adam one bright morning in early August. We drove to Drumnadrochit, a small town on the north side of Loch Ness, and then turned onto a narrow track that wound up the side of a steep hill overlooking the loch. We parked in a small gravel-lined bay at the top and walked across a narrow wooden bridge into Neil's compound.

The path led to a wooden building with a garish sign displaying the single word: 'Pottery'. Beyond it stood other wooden structures of variable age and solidity, where I guessed the denizens of Neil's retreat lived. Adam and I nosed around a little, but the place seemed deserted. We headed back to the pottery and found the door was ajar, so we went in. Tastefully arranged on the shelves were handmade plates and cups, colourfully painted and glazed. Adam was immediately drawn to a large teapot on a stand in the centre of the room. As he was admiring this object, a beautiful woman in her thirties came in through another door. Her short hair was dyed blonde, and her blue eyes sparkled as she greeted us.

'Hi, I'm Rebecca,' she said.

'Hi,' I said, 'my name's Dylan. I saw Neil speak at a

festival in England a couple of months ago. I've just moved up here, and I thought I'd pay him a visit.'

'Oh, I'm sorry,' she replied. 'I'm afraid Neil's not here at the moment.'

Neil, it turned out, was back in England at another festival. Rebecca was holding the fort on her own, the other members of Neil's rather depleted community having tagged along with him. I was disappointed, but Rebecca was very welcoming and showed us around the pottery, while I gently tried to glean more information about Goshem.

Rebecca had been living here for the past eighteen years, she said; all her adult life in fact, ever since she had first met Neil and come under his spell. But despite this rather sheltered existence she seemed perfectly friendly and not at all weird, so when we left an hour later, I was still unsure whether the dark stories circulating about Neil were true or just gossip run wild. I decided to return as soon as possible to find out.

Another community within striking distance of Utopia was Findhorn. Founded by three English eccentrics in a trailer park in 1962, the community is now home to more than four hundred people and has an international reputation. When I visited the place with Adam, a few days after going to Goshem, I was struck by the contrast.

The infrastructure was impressive. Beautifully made wooden houses in all kinds of shapes and colours nestled among luxuriant shrubbery, all kitted out with an array of green accoutrements – solar panels, wood pellet stoves, turf roofs and compost bins. In the distance several huge wind turbines were visible, generating so much electricity that a surplus was regularly exported to the National Grid.

But as we listened to our enthusiastic guide, the all-pervasive influence of the founders' bizarre spiritual ideology became increasingly apparent. The founders were originally told that nothing would grow in the harsh soil of the trailer park, the guide informed us, but they were nevertheless soon producing enormous vegetables. The appearance of these mighty cabbages was now a central part of Findhorn mythology, and attributed to supernatural causes, rather than to the substantial amount of horse manure that was donated by a local farmer. To this day, new arrivals at Findhorn are given careful instructions in how to speak to plants and 'tune into their higher overlighting spirits'.

All this claptrap disgusted me, but Adam was entranced. 'What if the same thing happens at Utopia?' he whispered, his eyes twinkling with hope. 'In forty years' time, they might be taking people on tours just like this, telling stories about us!'

The thought of going down in history as the founder of some kind of spiritual commune was frankly appalling. I was adamant that Utopia would be a secular community. That didn't mean religious people would not be allowed to join, of course; merely that we would studiously and steadfastly avoid giving any official sanction to any religious viewpoint.

The idea of religious neutrality proved to be the first sticking point with Adam. I was becoming alarmed by his increasingly frequent references to the 'Great Spirit' and other New Age-sounding concepts. I would soon learn this was a fundamental part of Adam's identity, but at the time it surprised me since I hadn't noticed it in our previous encounters. Had I unconsciously filtered out these references when we first met? Or had Adam carefully edited his manner of speaking so as not to scare me off? His frequent hypocrisy testified to a damning lack of insight – he would insist that all property was to be held in common, for example, but squirrel items of food away in his own yurt for his own personal consumption – but at times he could also be a wily bugger.

I decided to deal with the problem by sitting down with Adam one afternoon in August to figure out some basic rules for Utopia. But all I succeeded in doing was to open a can of worms.

We started by discussing our policy regarding visitors. We would welcome the occasional curious person, but we didn't want strangers continually traipsing through our little experiment. I knew Adam felt the same about this as I did, and I hoped that it would be easier to tackle the question of religion after we had established some degree of consensus.

'I'm not sure about the language you've used in framing some of the rules for Utopia,' I ventured.

My strategy didn't pay off. I could see Adam's back stiffen.

'What do you mean?' He eyed me suspiciously.

'Well,' I started, then paused, wondering exactly how to put this. 'Take the phrase "Great Spirit" for example.'

Adam's face darkened.

'When we were discussing the rules for meetings,' I continued, 'you suggested that people should "speak from the Great Spirit, and not from the ego". I think that way of putting things could alienate people who don't believe in the existence of a Great Spirit. It would be better if the rules for Utopia were expressed in terms that are religiously neutral.'

Adam wasn't at all happy with this suggestion. For him, the reference to the Great Spirit was essential if we were going to avoid selfishness and create a real sense of community. But I reminded him that the idea of religious neutrality had been central to the Utopia Experiment since its inception.

'Remember what I wrote on the website?' I asked.

Adam said nothing.

'About how the Utopia Experiment would be open to people of all religions and none? About how there wouldn't be any official ideology? To see if people with different beliefs can all get along? I don't want this place to be another Findhorn. It's hard to live there if you don't share their wacky beliefs about talking to plants.'

'There's nothing wrong with talking to plants,' said Adam, sulkily.

'OK, maybe not,' I said, 'but I don't want anyone to feel bad just because they don't believe plants can talk, or don't believe in God, or the Great Spirit. Can't we find a way to rephrase that stuff?'

'I don't see how.'

'Well don't you really mean that people should try to consider the good of the community before their own interests, and speak with the interests of the community at heart rather than their own private concerns?'

'I guess so,' said Adam.

But that wasn't really what he meant at all. As I would later discover, he had merely beaten a tactical retreat. In his mind, the Great Spirit was still very much alive, hovering above the experiment, and speaking exclusively through Adam.

In view of my growing misgivings about Adam, it was a relief when the second volunteer arrived. Agric had been the first person to apply for the experiment after I posted my brief announcement online. I had learned a lot from him and about him over the course of our hefty email correspondence since then, but this was the first time we had actually met. He pulled up around midday in his battered old Volkswagen camper van, packed with plants, gardening gear and other assorted implements. With his wispy white hair and impish expression, Agric seemed like another character out of Tolkien: if Adam was a deranged version of Gandalf, Agric was like a hobbit on speed – always fidgeting with something, or scampering over to some new activity with a mischievous grin on his face.

He seemed delighted to be here, and chatted excitedly as we walked down to the yurts together.

'Parts of the site are bigger than I expected. The stream area is a bit more wooded than I thought, too – and there are plenty of rowan trees for making rowanberry jelly. The land available for growing crops is flatter than I thought, which is good, but we'll have to move those pigs!'

The pigs, which Romay had kindly provided, were currently camped on the bit of land that Agric wanted to plant with a wide variety of crops: garlic, onions, Jerusalem artichokes, broad beans, spring cabbage, kale, mizuna, shallots and winter lettuce. I hoped that the pigs would soften up the ground in preparation for sowing the seeds.

Adam heard the chatter and poked his head out of his yurt. He smiled a broad grin and came out to give Agric a big bear hug, and the three of us sat down to make a fire and boil up some water for a cup of tea. Of course, there wouldn't be tea in Scotland after civilization collapsed – long-distance trade would take years to re-establish – but we told ourselves that we still had a stash of teabags left over from before the crash.

'We can make allowances for a few small pleasures, providing they fit with the scenario,' said Agric.

'Sure,' I nodded in agreement. 'But there are limits. We

can't just buy a crate of wine every week and tell ourselves that we keep finding well-stocked cellars in the abandoned farmhouses nearby. That would be rather implausible.'

Agric chuckled. 'Don't worry, we'll be making our own wine very soon.'

Adam grimaced. 'I don't think we should allow alcohol,' he said, sternly. 'This should be a pure place, for pure souls.'

'Oh, come on, Adam!' chirped Agric, amiably. 'We'll need an occasional drink to survive the apocalypse!'

It didn't take me long to realize that Agric was a fully committed doomer. For him, the scenario we were acting out at the Utopia Experiment was not just a collaborative fiction; it was preparation for the real thing. He could always back up his gloomy prognostications with lengthy discourses on the economy, climate change and, of course, peak oil. He'd even devised a scale for classifying different degrees of disaster.

At level one, collapse would involve a series of short-term interruptions to electric, gas and water supplies. Most of the basic infrastructure would be undamaged, and the financial system would remain intact, but many businesses would cease operation, leading to significant unemployment. It would be a crisis greater than anything experienced in the developed world in the last fifty years, and perhaps even worse than the Great Depression of the

1930s. It would be less locally devastating than severe floods or earthquakes, but much more widespread.

At level two, the international financial system would begin to creak at the seams, but it wouldn't collapse entirely. People would have to survive a few weeks or even months without regular access to gas, water and electricity, and shops would run low on food. Mortality rates would surge, reducing the population by up to 10 per cent, unless widespread lawlessness broke out, in which case more people would die, especially in areas with high population density.

At level three, much of the physical infrastructure would break down, and money would lose its value, but most critical damage could probably be repaired within a few months, or at most a couple of years. Developed countries would experience a huge reduction in their populations of up to 50 or 60 per cent. It would be like going back a hundred years, to the early twentieth century, but most important knowledge would probably be preserved.

Things get progressively worse with higher levels of collapse. By level five, which was the scenario we were attempting to simulate, the global population would be down by around 90 per cent, to less than a billion people. At level six, we would be down to only a hundred thousand, and we would all be living like hunter-gatherers again. By level seven there would be no people left at all. In Agric's words, the 'human experiment' would be 'terminated'.

The detail in which Agric had worked all this out fascinated me. There was a kind of grim pleasure in looking at such awful things so clinically, a feeling of staring disaster bravely in the face.

Nevertheless, there was also something that worried me about the precision in Agric's taxonomy, a kind of certainty about it all that smacked less of science than prophecy. A rash of books about global warming by some very eminent scientists had persuaded me that a belief in looming catastrophe was not necessarily a sign of insanity, but all the same, I couldn't help wondering if there were other factors, besides rational argument and empirical evidence, that lay behind Agric's conviction, and my own. In particular, I wondered why he seemed so cheerful when he charted the different levels of collapse. There was always a glint in his eye whenever he floated ideas about the likely date for the coming apocalypse, and it didn't seem to spring from the utopian idea that life after the crash would be more natural and healthy.

Eventually, it dawned on me that Agric was in the grip of what might be called 'Noah syndrome' – the smug anticipation of being able to say 'I told you so', when disaster finally arrives. It certainly makes it easier to endure the mocking glances of the majority, who view your preparations for the end of the world as the acts of a madman, if you can picture yourself sailing away in your ark as their heads sink beneath the waves. The idea that you see things as they really are, unlike the deluded masses, has an obvious attraction.

On the other hand, if Agric was so sure civilization was about to collapse, why hadn't he sold his house yet, like I had? Over the course of the next year, Agric would come and go, making the long drive up to Scotland from his home in Slough, and then back again after a month or so in Utopia. Before each journey south, he would declare that this time he would put his house up for sale and finally embrace the nomadic lifestyle he had been anticipating for so long. But he never did put it on the market. Perhaps, after all, he wasn't really as certain as he made out. Maybe he was just hedging his bets. I, on the other hand, was all in.

For almost the whole time I was in Utopia, I wore the same pair of faded blue combat trousers. They grew progressively baggier – and even more faded – as I helped Agric to clear the stones away from what would become our vegetable patch, and lost the extra pounds I had put on in the previous few years. Within a week of his arrival, Agric's clothes were as dirty as mine, and it was hard to tell by looking who had been here longer. Adam was never that clean to begin with, and the three of us would probably have smelled rotten, too, were it not for the fact that the pungent aroma of wood smoke clung to our clothes and masked every other odour.

We washed our clothes occasionally in the stream, which removed the mud but never seemed to erase the smell of wood smoke, and dried them in the sun, which blazed uncannily throughout most of August. I tried to imagine what it would be like when the winter set in and the rain lasted for days on end. Where would we dry our clothes? Would we even bother to wash them at all? And what would we do when our clothes began to fall apart?

'Anyone know how to make clothes?' I asked one day, as we sat around slurping Agric's homemade vegetable soup.

'Animal skins,' blurted out Agric. 'We need animal skins.'

'There are some deer around here,' said Adam, 'but the Great Spirit wouldn't want us to kill them.'

'The Great Spirit doesn't want us to get cold either,' I said.

'Deer hide would be great,' said Agric, authoritatively. 'We could use the hindquarter joint areas to make shoes and mittens and socks.'

'OK,' I said, 'but how are we going to kill a deer?'

'Dig a hole and put some wooden stakes in it,' beamed Agric. 'Nice sharp wooden stakes. And put a snare on top.'

'Then what?' I asked. 'I haven't got the faintest idea how to skin a deer.'

Agric wasn't fazed. 'We'll figure it out,' he said, wiping his mouth with the back of his hand and letting out a loud burp. 'How hard can it be?'

So that afternoon we set about building a deer trap. First we gathered some sticks about twelve inches long and sharpened the ends into fierce-looking points. Then we dug into some wet mud near the stream because Adam said he had noticed deer tracks there, and mud was easier to dig into anyway. The hole quickly filled up with water as we dug further down, and we got spattered with the brown liquid as we pounded the sticks into the earth. Finally, we made a snare from a spare guy rope, and laid it on top of the stakes, tying the other end tightly around a nearby tree. 'The stakes only help to get the snare tight around the animal's leg,' Agric told us. 'The rope is what's holding it.'

'We'd better not fall into the damn thing ourselves,' I muttered. An image of Adam, knee deep in the muddy hole, his thigh impaled on the tips of the wooden stakes, flashed into my mind. I wasn't sure this was such a good idea any more.

But I needn't have worried. No animal ever fell in to our makeshift deer trap, of either the four-legged or the two-legged variety. Every morning I would traipse down to inspect it, half wishing and half fearing to find an exhausted deer vainly struggling to free itself from the ever-tightening snare. And each time I would walk back to the yurts with a sigh of relief, glad I didn't have to cut the throat of a majestic and dangerous beast. A few weeks later a storm came and washed our little trap away.

Word arrived that Neil Oram had returned from his sojourn in England, and I determined to go back to

Goshem to meet the man about whom I had heard so much gossip.

This time, I went on my own. As I drove up the winding road, I began to wonder if I should have brought someone with me. What if Neil saw me as a threat to his pre-eminence, and didn't like the idea of another eccentric founding a rival community in his sphere of influence?

Rebecca was in the pottery, as if she hadn't moved since my previous visit. 'I'll go and get Neil,' she said.

A few minutes later, Neil appeared, smiling warmly and shaking my hand. His craggy face was framed by a bushy white beard and an embroidered smoking cap. He wore a faded Barbour jacket and old jeans tucked into yellow boots. His eyes twinkled with warmth and curiosity.

He didn't seem particularly dangerous, but I was still on my guard.

'Let's go for a walk,' said Neil.

The glint in his eye was hard to interpret. Regardless, I could hardly refuse his invitation. So the two of us trudged away from the pottery, past the other wooden buildings, and out into the woods. A few minutes later, we emerged from trees to find ourselves on the edge of a steep slope overlooking Loch Ness. The air was humid, and the sunlight only emerged here and there from the light grey clouds, but the view was breathtaking all the same. It was a beautiful, haunting place, and I could see why Neil had chosen to settle here. It was a world apart, beyond the reach of the law, where Neil ruled supreme over his little band of followers.

Neil asked me about Utopia, and told me how he'd moved to the Highlands in 1968 and squatted on this land, which, according to some ancient law, he now legally owned by virtue of continuous occupation. We discussed classical music, philosophy and poetry. He had a highly cultivated mind, though he wore his erudition lightly, and made provocative, if sometimes obscure, connections between apparently unrelated ideas. It was the best conversation I had had for months.

So we returned, without incident, to the ramshackle buildings that formed the heart of his empire, and Neil made me a cup of tea in the wooden hut where he slept.

'So how are you going to fund Utopia?' he asked.

'I'm using the proceeds from selling my house,' I said.

Neil's eyes widened in surprise.

'Are you paying for everything yourself? Don't your volunteers have to contribute anything? You are feeding them, housing them, all out of your own pocket?'

I nodded, puzzled by Neil's focus on the financial side of things.

Neil shook his head. 'It sounds like you are buying friends,' he said.

I hadn't thought of it that way before, but he had a point. It did rather smack of desperation. And it wasn't even a good deal. For the volunteers weren't my friends at all. They were my lab rats, mere material for my experiment. Or robots, perhaps. But what did that make me? Was I a scientist, doing real research? Or was I some kind of sociopath, callously playing with people's lives? The more I thought about it, the more I worried it was the latter.

8. WINTER

By September the days were getting noticeably shorter and the sky was increasingly overcast. Whether due to the lack of light, or to the weeks of hoeing and digging, I was beginning to feel weak and tired and lonely. I wasn't eating properly either; by the time I stopped work for lunch I was usually too tired to cook, and there were too few of us to organize a cooking rota, so I would end up simply eating a few slices of Agric's homemade bread, which was delicious, but nowhere near enough to keep me well fed. I began to lose weight.

As my mood darkened, the thought that Bo would soon be joining me became sweeter. Over the course of the past few months our relationship had evolved into something more substantial. She had paid me a couple of visits and we had gradually developed plans for her to come and live with me in Utopia.

I had originally envisaged sharing a yurt with her and her daughter, but the idea of raising a young child in such primitive conditions proved unpalatable to Bo, so we eventually decided that I would rent a cottage for them not far from the experiment. The problems with this plan were as obvious to my friends as they were imperceptible to me. Romay in particular would often try to warn me that the experiment would require every ounce of my energy and attention if it was to succeed, and that the presence of a girlfriend – not to mention a young child – would be a serious distraction. But I wouldn't listen. I was still filled with a feeling of invincibility.

As autumn wound on, I came to think of Bo less as someone I could save – from London, from the collapse of civilization – and more as someone who could save me. I mistook my exhaustion and neediness for the pain of separation. I looked forward to seeing her with a kind of feverish longing, and imagined that everything would be right again when she finally arrived.

In late September, a few days before my fortieth birthday, Bo drove up from London with her daughter. I was waiting at the little cottage I had rented for them a few miles away from Utopia. It was a pretty basic affair, with a kitchen, bathroom and living room downstairs, and two bedrooms upstairs, but I had tried to make it as cosy as I could. Bo was exhausted but happy, and after she had put her daughter to bed, we lit a fire in the open fireplace in the living room. It felt strange to be back in a house again after spending so many evenings outside, or sheltering in my yurt, but it was nice not to have to worry about the wind or the rain. We opened a bottle of wine and drank a toast to this new chapter in our lives.

'I'm so glad I'm finally here,' said Bo.

'I know!' I said, savouring the first wine I had tasted for months. 'Let's throw a feast to celebrate your arrival and my birthday! I'm going to kill one of the pigs and roast it whole!'

Bo chuckled and looked at me with a faint air of scepticism.

'Do you know how to kill a pig?' she asked.

'My friend Todd said he would help out whenever we needed him,' I replied.

Todd had lived in the Highlands for over thirty years. He was short and wiry, with deep blue eyes and a short brown beard, and seemed to possess the full range of skills required to survive in the wilderness. The following day, on Todd's advice, I moved one of the pigs into another pen, out of sight of his compadres, a few days before the fateful hour, so he would be used to his new surroundings and thus not be anxious when we were about to kill him. We had named him Fatso because he had put on more weight than any of his companions.

On the appointed morning, Todd came over with his rifle. I went and filled a bucket with scraps for the pigs as usual, and when Fatso stuck his head in it, Todd pointed his gun at the unsuspecting animal's brain, the muzzle half an inch away from his skull, and pulled the trigger. Fatso closed his eyes and fell over, and some blood ran out of his nose. His body twitched for ages.

I felt sick. I had been pretty blasé about the thought of killing Fatso in the previous few days, but now I realized it had all been a sham, and that I had actually been dreading it. I tried to put on a brave face as I helped Todd carry Fatso's body into the potato shed and string it up. We stuck a big metal hook through each hind leg, ran some rope through the hooks and over a lintel, and pulled hard until Fatso was dangling face down. Todd cut Fatso's throat, and when all the blood had run out into a bucket, we took the body down again and laid it out on a big table. Then we covered it in hessian sacks, and for the next few hours we poured pan after pan of boiling water on the carcass to loosen up the bristles. But no matter how much water we poured, we couldn't shave them off with our knives, so eventually we gave up and burnt them off with a blowtorch.

Finally, when the last bristles were gone, we stuck a big spit right through Fatso's hairless body, so it went in through his arse and came out of his open mouth. Then we threaded loops of heavy-duty twine through Fatso's back all the way down the length of his spine, tying it tightly to the spit so he wouldn't flop around as we turned it. We each grabbed hold of one end of the spit and lifted it onto the stakes we had driven into the ground either side of the fire pit. We had lit the fire while we were shaving Fatso, and now the wood had burnt down to glowing red-black embers that gave off a flameless smoky heat. For the rest of the day, Todd kept the coals alive, feeding the fire pit now and again with new embers from another fire that was fed in turn with fresh blocks of wood. Every ten minutes or so we would turn the spit a little, to ensure Fatso got a nice even tan all over, until darkness had fallen.

Todd sliced deeply into the body to check it was thoroughly cooked, and when he nodded his head in approval I piled in the remaining coals, to raise a final blast of heat. When Fatso's skin began to crackle and bubble and blister, Todd peeled off a little and handed it to me to taste. It felt strange to be eating the animal we had cared for those past few months, and fed that very morning, but it was delicious, and the crackling melted in my mouth.

'Thank you, Fatso,' I whispered, and called everyone over to join us.

Soon we were all sitting round the fire pit in a big circle, tucking in to succulent pieces of pork and crunchy bits of crackling, and big hunks of freshly baked bread, all washed down with some red wine that Todd had brought with him. Next to me sat Bo, looking much more relaxed than when she had arrived, with her daughter beside her, her clothes caked in dirt and pig fat smeared round her mouth. Agric was deep in conversation with Todd, quizzing him on the finer points of butchery. Romay had joined us too, and had a big smile on her face, relieved to see that the experiment seemed to be going so well. Adam was lost in his own thoughts, seemingly savouring every morsel of the meat, having declared that the Great Spirit had given him a temporary dispensation from his holy commitment to vegetarianism.

I sat back and closed my eyes. I could feel the warmth

from the coals on my face. What a wonderful way to end the summer and celebrate my fortieth birthday. Bo was here, and the experiment was off to a good start. Two yurts now stood proudly by the river alongside an open-air wooden platform that Adam had built without knowing quite what it was for; it now served as a place to cook and eat lunch. The pigs had done a good job of preparing the ground for Agric's vegetable patch, and we had begun to renovate the potato shed – which for some reason we all now referred to as the Barn – with the intention of turning it into a kitchen, dining area and general indoor workspace.

I smiled to myself and thanked my lucky stars for saving me from civilization, and bringing me to this wonderful wild place. All my autumn blues had faded away, and I was happy again. Now Bo was here, I would be able to face the winter ahead with renewed strength and enthusiasm.

In October we had some of the heaviest rainfall and strongest winds that the Highlands had seen for many years. At one point the chimney pipes blew off both the yurts – but that was the worst of the damage, and it was easily fixed. I was very pleased that the yurts had survived such extreme weather. If they could survive that, they should be robust enough to last throughout the experiment.

The winds also brought down some big branches

from the older trees. A couple of them blocked the path leading down to the yurts, and it took three of us to drag them out of the way. They made excellent firewood; I spent an hour or two every day sawing them into blocks and then splitting the blocks with an axe. Chopping wood was fun, even though I soon discovered there was an art to it that I was far from mastering. It was in those moments, when I swung the axe in the cold autumn air, that I felt happiest at Utopia, not just because of the satisfying thwack that came when the axe cleaved the block right down the middle, but also because I could finally believe I had left my academic life far behind me, and transformed myself into a strapping backwoodsman.

Agric and I put up some more fencing to make a new enclosure for the pigs so we could move them off their old, well-dug area, which we planned to use for our first vegetable garden. When we had finally succeeded in moving them, however, we found the ground was still soaked after the heavy rains and too wet to plant. So we had to dig another bit of ground nearby without the help of our porcine friends. Digging was not nearly so much fun as chopping wood, and I soon grew weary of it. There were lots of stones in the soil, and it was a thankless task to pick them all out, but Agric was patient and tireless, and would carry on turning the clods of earth long after I had given up. By the end of the month, the patch of land was finally ready to start planting our winter crop.

We sowed broad beans, garlic, onions and shallots.

Meanwhile, Adam worked alone on a little heart-shaped herb garden down by the yurts. I wasn't sure whether the herbs would grow outdoors throughout the winter months, but there was no dissuading him. He planted sage, parsley, lemongrass, rosemary, oregano, mint and thyme. In the middle he drove a wooden stake with a sign declaring it to be the Heart Garden, the sacred heart of Utopia. Nearby, at the base of a tree, another sign read: 'The Mighty Oak – King of Utopia'.

'What on earth is that all about?' I asked, one afternoon, when the rain was falling so heavily that we had been forced to take refuge in one of the yurts.

'We must honour the oak trees here,' replied Adam, gravely. 'They could be our last hope.'

'How come?' I asked, not following his gist at all.

'It's the perfect wood for boat building,' he replied. 'We can cut planks and bend them with steam.'

'That sounds like a lot of work,' I said. 'But maybe we can try it later on.'

'I think we should start soon,' said Adam. 'Look how hard it's raining.'

'I'm sorry,' I said, scratching my head. 'I don't see the connection.'

Adam paused a minute before replying. 'Climate change!' he exclaimed. 'Global warming. There's going to be a lot more water around. Sea levels are rising. We've got to have a plan B, in case Utopia gets flooded.'

'You mean like a lifeboat or something?' I ventured.

Adam shook his head solemnly. 'Not a lifeboat,' he said. 'An ark. We've got to build an ark.'

I blinked, dumbfounded by this radical proposal.

'You mean like in the Bible?' I spluttered.

'Precisely,' said Adam, without batting an eyelid. 'We can have it ready and waiting, so when the sea levels rise, we can all get in and let the tides carry us away.'

'And are we going to collect breeding pairs of all the local fauna?' I smirked, wondering how far he intended to take the biblical analogy.

'Of course not! There won't be space for all of them. But we should definitely take a few pigs.'

He paused for a moment, lost in thought. Then he nodded, as if agreeing with a suggestion from the Great Spirit.

'The pigs will show us the way,' he said.

In November I left for a few days to attend the Free Thinking Festival organized by the BBC in Liverpool, where I spoke in a debate about the future of civilization. One of the other panellists was my old friend Nick Bostrom, who had introduced me to the Unabomber the year before.

During a coffee break, Nick asked me a question that has stuck in my mind ever since: 'How likely do you think it is that something like the imaginary scenario you are acting out in Scotland might really come to pass in the next ten years?' I paused for thought. 'Give me your answer as a percentage,' Nick added, crucially. I thought a bit longer, and finally declared that I thought that the chance of such a thing happening within the next ten years was about 50 per cent.

Nick looked shocked. Not even the most pessimistic scientists thought things were that bad. In his 2003 book *Our Final Century*, the astronomer Martin Rees put the chance of a major global catastrophe this century at 50 per cent. Assuming the risk is more or less constant during the whole century, the chance of such a catastrophe happening in any given decade works out at just under 7 per cent. That was an order of magnitude less than my 50 per cent estimate. To put it the other way round, my estimate of 50 per cent for the decade implied a 99.9 per cent chance of such a catastrophe happening this century, which made Rees look positively sanguine by comparison.

Whenever I have looked back on the experiment since then, I have often recalled Nick's incisive question, and my overconfident answer. The nice thing about Nick's question was his insistence that I put a number on my estimate. He didn't let me get away with some vague expression such as 'quite likely'. And as a result, I could see all the more clearly how wrong I was. The British economist John Maynard Keynes famously said that he would rather be vaguely right than precisely wrong. But here, the precision that Nick had demanded of me forced me to own up to my error in a way that vagueness never would. It betrayed the extent to which what had started out in my mind as an exercise in collaborative fiction had already become an insurance policy against a global disaster that I was increasingly convinced was imminent.

In December we killed another pig, but this time we didn't throw a feast. This meat would have to last a lot longer, and keep us going throughout the rest of the winter. Todd came over again and showed us how to butcher the animal. Once the head was removed, the carcass split open, and the outer layer of fat and skin removed from the hams, we left it hanging in the Barn to chill in the cold night air. Meat should never be cut up and cured until all the animal heat is out, Todd explained, and he promised to return the next day to help us with the salting and curing.

The following morning Todd came back with a fearsome set of instruments. He sawed, sliced and peeled the carcass into increasingly smaller pieces, often asking one of us to hold it steady as he did so. Agric was always very happy to volunteer, which spared me the gruesome task. Adam looked on disapprovingly. The Great Spirit had insisted he return to his strict vegetarian diet, and now forbade him from even touching meat.

Within a few hours the once proud animal was reduced to neat piles of bacon, chops, ribs, hams, and a couple of buckets of scraps – one containing lumps of fat, and the other, trimmings for making sausages. We then proceeded to salt the meat, taking handfuls of the coarse crystals and massaging them into the surface of the cold slimy pieces of pork as our palms became as sticky and glistening as the meat itself. We planned to build a cold room by digging an underground pit, but that would have to wait until more volunteers arrived. For now, we just left it in the coldest end of the Barn, as far away from the kitchen as possible. We had nailed up some sheets of plywood to form a thin dividing wall so the smell of the cured pork wouldn't stink out the rest of the Barn, which was now where we spent most of our time during the day, whenever we weren't chopping wood or feeding the pigs.

But that was not the end of the pig process. There remained one more step before we could safely leave the meat in storage over the rest of the winter months, and that was to smoke it. Todd had built us a cold smoker for precisely this purpose, and he brought it over a few days later for our final lesson in meat preservation. It was an odd-looking contraption, which Todd had welded together from bits and pieces of old metal containers and painted matt black to finish. Two boxes were connected by a single tube about the same size as a toilet roll. The first box was smaller than the second, in which we hung the hams and bacon from a couple of thin horizontal poles. We made a fire in the first box, and the smoke then passed through the tube into the second box and gradually infused the meat that was hanging there. This was called 'cold smoking', Todd informed us, because the meat didn't hang directly over the fire, as in hot smoking, but sat in a separate container, thus absorbing the smoke but not the heat.

Todd had brought some little bags of woodchips with him from a variety of trees: oak, hickory, apple and cherry. He soaked some of the cherry woodchips in water and then scattered them on the fire. Within a few minutes they were steaming and spitting and giving off a sweet-smelling smoke. We kept this going for about four or five hours, by which time our mouths were watering with anticipation. Most of the meat would go straight into storage, but we couldn't resist trying some right away.

It did not disappoint. The meat was dry but chewy, salty but with a smoky sweetness. We thanked Todd for teaching us and for the cold smoker he had built, and gave him some bacon and ham in return. The rest of the meat we hung in the cold end of the Barn to keep us going for the rest of the winter. But it didn't last as long as we hoped. Compared with the trouble of going fishing or hunting for roadkill, it was always much easier to raid our precious store of pork and simply throw some of it in the oven. And within a week or two it was all gone.

Snow doesn't tend to settle on the Black Isle. Indeed, some say the place derives its name from the fact that, viewed from a distance, the dark earth stands out in winter against the whiteness of the surrounding country-side. Closer up, you can see that there is in fact a light dusting of snow, like the faintest trace of icing sugar sprinkled on plum pudding. And that is enough to transform the place into something out of fairyland.

The earth was hard and solid, a welcome relief from the sloshy mud that we had trudged through during the previous months, but the trees were now bare, and provided no protection against the fierce wind that seemed to blow right through our clothes as if we had none, no matter how many layers we wore. The only way to keep warm was to keep active, by chopping wood or carrying water or tightening the ropes on the yurt. Or to stoke up the stoves, tie down the canvas flaps that served as doors, and take refuge inside the yurts for hours on end, until your muscles cried out for exercise, or your bladder could wait no more.

But there was also work to do on the Barn. We rescued an old Rayburn from a derelict cottage and set it against the back wall. It had two hotplates and one small oven, and burned wood. It also had a back boiler for heating water, so we plumbed in a header tank to feed it, and a storage cylinder to keep the hot water that rose up the pipe from the boiler. We had to make sure the header tank was continually topped up, which meant frequent trips to fetch water from the stream, but the effort was worth it for the luxury of hot water on tap. It wasn't enough for a bath, and we didn't have a bathtub anyway, only a barrel that we had sawn in half and which was rarely emptied of the fetid water we occasionally stepped into to rinse ourselves down. But it made all the difference when it came to washing the dishes, especially after making porridge.

Cleaning the cold sticky oatmeal off the pan and bowls had been a thankless task in ice cold water. The glue just seemed to stick harder, clinging to whatever implement you used to scrape the pan, and then sticking to the thing you used to scrape that, so that you only succeeded in transferring the muck from one item to the next. We didn't have detergent either, since apparently that had all run out when civilization collapsed, and we couldn't use rags, since we had a limited supply of them and didn't want to clog them all up with glutinous sludge. In the end we'd got used to a thin layer of slime covering the pans and bowls. But now we had hot water on tap, and could actually get the pans shining clean again. I had never been so happy to do the washing up.

Hard though it was to live in such primitive conditions in wintertime, it felt authentic, and satisfying, and wholesome. It was what I had dreamed about all those months while I put in place the plans for Utopia, between coming back from Mexico and heading up to Scotland. But there was one thing I hadn't foreseen, and that was Bo. She was living in the little cottage I had rented for her, and I would head over to see her every day or two, and then I would stay the night. I felt pulled in opposite directions, torn between my desire to spend time with Bo and my wish to tough it out in Utopia, to see if I could weather the whole winter in such rudimentary conditions. Whenever I was at Utopia I would worry about Bo, and whenever I was with Bo I would feel like I was cheating, sneaking off to a warm cottage while Adam shivered in his yurt, or Agric chopped wood. They never said a word. Indeed, Agric would tell me to go and spend time with Bo, that she needed me, and he could cope just fine without me. I felt guilty, and I longed to feel the cold with him, to suffer and rejoice in the harsh simplicity of it all.

But when I awoke in the cottage, I never felt such gratitude for a hot shower, and as that steaming water cascaded over my body, I would think about how wonderful technology was, and how in days gone by only kings and lords would have had the pleasure of regular hot baths, and how this little shower was the mechanical equivalent of a dozen servants, who would have worked and sweated for hours to collect the firewood, to heat large cauldrons of water, to race upstairs with steaming buckets, to fill the king's tub. And when I got back to Utopia an hour later, to find Adam still frozen into his sleeping bag, and Agric shivering as he tried to light the Rayburn, I would feel very grateful that I didn't have to spend every morning like that myself.

But when we cooked breakfast on the Rayburn, I would change my mind. It took ages for the Rayburn to heat up, but our omelette and beans tasted all the more delicious for taking so long to prepare. And whenever I headed off again to visit Bo, it would be hard to leave, with the smell of freshly baked bread wafting out of the oven, and Adam darning his socks by candlelight, and Agric chopping vegetables for supper – and a sense of betrayal gnawing away at my heart.

I had built not one but two little communities, and yet I was not fully a member of either. Romay continued to warn me I was asking for trouble, and that I would have to choose between them, or mess up both. I continued to ignore her warnings, assuring her that everything would be fine, that I had enough time and energy to care for both my new families. 'Yes,' Romay would say, 'you do now, but the experiment has just begun, and there are only two volunteers here. Things will be very different when spring comes, and Utopia begins to grow again.'

I still cherished the fantasy that Bo might move to Utopia in the spring. Perhaps she would no longer feel the need for walls of brick and mortar when the worst of the winter weather was over. And then my attention would no longer be divided, and my two little families would become one big tribe.

So I asked Bo to marry me.

I'd already been married once, in my twenties, and had decided never to marry again, but now I had gone and proposed, and Bo had accepted. In January, as the wedding approached, Romay was worrying about what effect this further complication would have on my experiment. Again I dismissed her concerns with a smug assurance that all would be fine, and busied myself with preparations.

Finally, the big day arrived. It was a sunny morning in February and I felt on top of the world. Bo had invited some of her friends from London, and I had invited my mother and sister. The two of them flew up to Scotland the day before, and I can still remember the look of horror on their faces when I proudly showed them the site of my experiment.

Charlotte peered reluctantly into one of the yurts. A couple of sleeping bags lay crumpled on the hard wooden floor, while various items of clothing hung limply from the hazel roof poles, reeking of wood smoke from the stove in the centre.

'You sleep here? In this mess?' she asked, screwing her face up as if she was sucking on a slice of lemon.

'Well, I do spend a couple of nights a week at the cottage with Bo,' I said.

'I would spend every night there, if I were you,' said Charlotte. 'This is horrible.'

My mother was equally unimpressed, though she seemed more sorry for me than appalled by the primitive conditions in which the utopians slept. She was even sadder that I was getting married. She thought I was getting married for the wrong reasons and therefore risked making a terrible mistake, and had no hesitation in telling me so. She had not wanted to come, but I had begged her, and she had taken a week off from a three-month stint in southern Spain to attend the ceremony.

The day itself seems unreal to me when I recall it now. I can remember standing in a registry office in the nearest town, with Bo next to me and a motley crew of guests seated behind us. I was smiling, and dressed in a shabby suit I had retrieved from a musty case of clothes, unopened since I packed up my house in the Cotswolds some eight months before. And there was Bo, looking fabulous in a pretty white dress.

And yet I see this scene from the outside, as if I were an observer looking on from a distance, not from the perspective of the man who made his vows that day. I cannot see inside his head or divine what is really driving him, as he slips a wedding ring on the woman's finger, and presumably kisses her. All I feel is a shiver down my own spine, the spine of the observer, since I know what happens next.

9. POSITIVE DISINTEGRATION

I had been in the hospital for about two weeks when Vera arrived on the ward. She was by far the maddest person I met while I was there. You could have a conversation of some description with all the other patients, but not with Vera. If you asked her a question, she would say something completely unrelated in reply, or start jabbering about her wedding ring, while staring right past your face into the space behind your head. Within half an hour of her arrival, nobody bothered even trying to speak to her any more. So Vera just sat around, fidgeting compulsively, whispering to herself, crying, and occasionally shouting out loud.

For some reason, Rowena seemed particularly annoyed by Vera's behaviour. Everybody else just ignored her, but on those rare occasions when Rowena emerged from her room, she would glower at Vera and tell her to shut up. There were times when I thought Rowena was going to walk over and punch her.

But Rowena somehow managed to control herself and walk away. Until, that is, she was seated at the same table as Vera one evening for supper. I was chewing silently on the unappetizing sausages that had been served up, trying to ignore Vera while she nagged away at some unseen companion, when all of a sudden Rowena picked up her fork and threw it like a dagger at Vera's face. It somersaulted through the air and in an instant the prongs embedded themselves in the flesh just above Vera's left eyebrow.

There was a moment of silence as Vera stopped talking and we all looked in astonishment at the fork sticking out of her forehead, quivering gently, as thick dark drops of blood began to trickle down her face. And then Vera started screaming, a shrill ear-splitting scream. Rowena stood up, glowered at Vera in triumph, and marched off to her room. I was dumbstruck.

Suddenly, the hospital didn't seem like such a safe place after all. After the first few days of not knowing what to expect, of my imagination conjuring up all sorts of fearful images of evil psychiatrists and brutal nurses, I had gradually calmed down, until the place began to feel dependable and protective – safer and saner than Utopia, anyway. And now, in an instant, that sense of security was suddenly snatched away, and the hospital felt as dangerous and unpredictable as anywhere else. There was no refuge, not even here, no place to hide from random violence, no guarantee that, when you least expected it, a fork wouldn't skewer your forehead, or even perhaps your eye. But the danger didn't come from the obviously mad ones. It came from the quiet ones, the ones who kept themselves to themselves.

It was my weekly chat with Dr Satoshi. I was fidgeting as usual, picking at my face compulsively and clicking my heels together every now and again as I sat opposite him, feeling ashamed of every tic, but unable to keep still.

'Have you ever heard of Kazimierz Dabrowski?' he asked.

I shook my head.

'He was a Polish psychiatrist. He wrote about something called positive disintegration.'

That last word made me wince. I had fallen apart and it didn't feel very positive at all. No, I hadn't *fallen* apart – it was all my own work. I had dismantled my whole life, bit by bit. I had systematically deconstructed everything I had built up over the past decade – my career, my relationships, my lifestyle. I had burnt all my bridges, alienated my former colleagues, sold my house, and given away most of my possessions. The few remaining ones lay scattered about Utopia or stuffed in cardboard boxes in a shipping container at the edge of a muddy field. I hadn't realized until then how our most cherished possessions are like extensions of our bodies, and now it felt as though I had dismembered my very self. I had taken an axe to my carefully arranged existence and smashed it into a thousand pieces.

'What's positive about disintegration?' I muttered glumly.

'You should know,' smiled Dr Satoshi.

'What do you mean?' I asked.

'Well, isn't your whole experiment about finding Utopia after collapse? Sometimes you have to take something apart in order to construct something better.'

I pondered his remark for a moment. 'Like a snake that has to shed its skin in order to grow?' I ventured, hesitantly.

'Yes, exactly! People who never experience a crisis don't advance. But Dabrowski thought people have different potential for growth. The ones who can go furthest tend to be oversensitive. They feel the extremes of joy and sorrow more deeply than others. They display what some call *emotional intensity*.'

'For a long time I thought everyone was like that,' I said, slightly embarrassed by how naive I must have been.

'Well they aren't. You are a very unusual person, Dylan, and you have a lot more to accomplish in your life.'

'But I've ruined everything,' I said. 'What can I do now?'

Dr Satoshi paused for a minute and looked at me seriously.

'You'll just have to start again,' he said.

I groaned. I barely had the energy to get out of bed in the morning, let alone rebuild my whole life. The idea seemed impossibly daunting.

'Tell me more about this positive disintegration thing,' I murmured.

Dr Satoshi leaned back in his chair. 'Dabrowski distinguished between two levels of psychological development,' he began. 'At the first level, which he called primary integration, people largely accept the values and customs of the society in which they have grown up. It hardly even crosses their minds that there might be other ways of doing things and alternative value systems.'

'You mean they are like robots,' I interjected. 'They're just blindly following the program that society has installed in them.'

'Exactly!' smiled Dr Satoshi. 'According to Dabrowski, most people stay like this all their lives. A few people, however, rebel against their programming. Dabrowski thought these individuals suffered from things that most psychologists would regard as unhealthy: a tendency towards depression, dissatisfaction with oneself, feelings of inferiority and guilt, states of anxiety, inhibitions, and over-excitability. Dabrowski didn't see these as necessarily bad things, however. On the contrary, he saw them as valuable spurs to psychological development.'

'Why's that?' I asked.

'Because they can prompt you to question the customs and values which you've previously taken for granted. By making you feel different, cut off from the society around you, these "pathological" traits actually prepare the way for psychological growth.'

Now my curiosity was aroused. 'It's an interesting idea,' I said.

'Here, take this,' said Dr Satoshi, handing me a small book. It was a collection of Dabrowski's writings, and over the course of the next few days I managed to plough through the first two chapters. Reading was still difficult, but my concentration was beginning to improve, and every time my mind drifted I would patiently try to bring it back again and take in another few sentences.

I learned that, for Dabrowski, psychological growth is always painful, because it involves dismantling the program that has governed one's thoughts and actions since childhood. This process of disintegration often involves some kind of nervous breakdown, a genuine period of mental illness. And this is by no means always positive. Dabrowski was not some naive forebear of the anti-psychiatry movement; he recognized that disintegration could be, and often is, purely negative. What enables one person to learn from the experience of disintegration and emerge reborn from the storm of mental illness, while another sinks beneath the waves forever, is a mystery, and there is no way of knowing which of these fates awaits you as the storm brews. But equally there is no way of growing without sailing right into the heart of that tempest. Sometimes it may appear that you have no choice; the wind blows you into the storm willy-nilly. But Dabrowski thought that it was also possible for the individual to become an active agent in his disintegration, and even breakdown, if he so wished.

Is that what I had done? Had I driven myself mad on purpose? For the previous twelve months I had made it my business to think constantly about the collapse of civilization, all day and all night long. And I think I sensed beforehand that this was a psychologically dangerous thing to do, yet wanted to do it anyway, just to see what would happen.

Maybe an unflinching focus on the end of the world is a kind of test, like Nietzsche's eternal return of the same, which only those who are truly happy can pass, and which sends everyone else mad. Or maybe Dabrowski was right, and one way to attain true happiness is by going through a kind of artificially induced madness, like a rite of passage or spiritual exercise. And maybe that is the point: to terrify yourself to the point where you are no longer terrified, to stare into the abyss until you no longer suffer from vertigo – or until you topple over the edge, and feel the rush of air around you as you fall, with not even the consolation of knowing you will one day hit the ground and put an end to your fear for ever.

To emerge from this dark night of the soul, said Dabrowski, one must develop a new value system, one that is truly yours, not the prefabricated morality pushed onto us by society. 'Thus the person finds a "cure" for himself,' he wrote, 'not in the sense of a rehabilitation but rather in the sense of reaching a higher level than the one at which he was prior to disintegration.' Some forms of mental illness, then, provide an opportunity to finally take one's life in one's own hands. 'They are expressive,' wrote Dabrowski, 'of a drive for psychic autonomy, especially moral autonomy, through transformation of a more or less primitively integrated structure.'

Is that what I was beginning to do now, in hospital? Was this my opportunity finally to learn to stand on my own two feet? I was beginning to wonder whether, in setting up the Utopia Experiment, I had perhaps been trying to avoid confronting my demons on my own. Perhaps some part of me already knew, before the idea for the experiment first occurred to me, that I was sliding into a depression, and the experiment was simply a misguided attempt to create some kind of 'therapeutic community' in which I could seek refuge. But in the end, it didn't work. The community wasn't therapeutic at all. On the contrary, it just made things worse, and now, at last, I was finally on my own.

The process of reconstruction, of creating a new self, I realized, was a solitary one. Other people may poke and prod you along, but it is ultimately down to you. You can't create a unique self by following someone else's path. You must find your way out of the storm on your own.

It is precisely because it is so isolating that mental illness plays such a crucial role in the process. If constructing a unique persona and developing your own set of values is a fundamentally solitary act, madness helps by driving others away from you, and pitching you into an empty black hole. This is to suggest that the madness comes first, and leads to separation, but in fact things work the other way round too. The human need to belong is so powerful that when a person ceases to be part of a community to which he had previously felt he belonged, the process of disaffiliation can itself damage his mental health. Hence madness and isolation work together in a mutually reinforcing pattern, each in turn exacerbating the other.

When lonely people join cults, they often experience a rapid improvement in their mental health, as the new community provides the long-sought social acceptance they had previously been lacking, a phenomenon known as the 'relief effect'. But this of course blocks any chance of real growth, as the new member submits to another foreign program and relinquishes the search for individuality. For some people, perhaps, that is the best they can hope for. Not everyone has the strength, or the luck, to sail helplessly through the stormy waters on his own. But that is the only way to become truly yourself.

One day Romay came to visit me in hospital. She brought me some books to read and some sweets. She remarked on how nice my room was.

'You should have seen the old asylum. It was an old Victorian building. No private rooms with en suite bathrooms there!'

I had, in fact, seen the old asylum. A few days before, a nurse had taken a few of us out on a walk in the surrounding countryside, and the path led us right past the building. Some renovation work was underway to convert the main complex into luxury apartments, but the untouched parts of the building showed how gloomy and forbidding it must have been when it housed the local madmen. Imposing square towers thrust upwards from the thick stone walls, crowned by spiky roofs of dark slate. Angus McPhee, an outsider artist, spent almost half a century here, silently weaving hats, pouches and harnesses from grass, sheep wool and beech leaves, in his own private form of art therapy. A few months after I visited, the place was burnt down by a couple of teenagers. I can't say I blame them.

Romay seemed to find my situation rather comical. Here I was, in a nice warm building, being fed three square meals a day, while the volunteers toiled away at the fields and slept in windy yurts. She didn't seem to believe I was really ill. She even seemed to resent me being there, though she smiled and laughed and made light of the situation. Maybe she thought I was malingering. I was too confused to try and persuade her otherwise, but I was deeply upset by her apparent lack of empathy or understanding.

One of the books that Romay brought me to read in hospital was *The Blank Slate* by Steven Pinker. I had read it several years before, when it was first published, and I turned to it again like an old friend.

But old friends do not just give solace. They can also

confront you with harsh truths. And there, right in chapter one, the book did just that.

Pinker begins by describing two contrasting views of human nature. On the one hand, there is 'the belief that humans in their natural state are selfless, peaceable, and untroubled, and that blights such as greed, anxiety, and violence are the products of civilization'. By contrast, humans have also been seen as naturally nasty, selfish and violent. Pinker uses the philosophers Rousseau and Hobbes as dramatis personae to represent each of these views. He recognizes that their actual writings are more complex than this stark contrast suggests, but as a rhetorical device it is broadly correct.

'Much depends,' Pinker argues, 'on which of these armchair anthropologists is correct.' And later on in the book, he tells us whom he thinks that is:

> . . . many intellectuals have embraced the image of peaceable, egalitarian, and ecology-loving natives. But in the past two decades anthropologists have gathered data on life and death in pre-state societies rather than accepting the warm and fuzzy stereotypes. What did they find? In a nutshell: Hobbes was right, Rousseau was wrong.

Pinker backs up this verdict with startling evidence concerning homicide rates in contemporary hunter-gatherer societies. The Jivaro people in northern Peru and eastern Ecuador are famous for their head-hunting raids. A band of men from one camp attack a homestead in another camp, killing the men, spearing the older women to death, and taking younger women as their brides. Up to 60 per cent of male deaths are due to warfare. In the Yanomami, who inhabit the Amazon rainforest, it's around 40 per cent. In the US and Europe, the figure for the whole of the twentieth century is less than 2 per cent, and that includes the dead of both world wars and Vietnam. Rousseau blamed violence on civilization, but it now seems clear that advanced industrial societies are a lot more peaceful than pre-agricultural ones. Hobbes was right to describe life in the state of nature as one of 'continual fear and danger of violent death', and 'nasty, brutish, and short'.

And while I was rereading Pinker, I suddenly remembered something I had written as I was preparing for the Utopia Experiment:

> If we ask which of these two thinkers, Hobbes or Rousseau, is more supported by the scientific evidence that has come in over the past century, then the answer is absolutely clear. Rousseau was much more accurate than Hobbes. When we look at the evidence, it turns out that the idea of the noble savage is both lovely and true. It is Hobbes, and all the other cynics, who are wrong. Our savage ancestors were nobler than us, and indisputably happier.

But what struck me, even more than the obvious contradiction between my verdict and Pinker's, was the remarkable amnesia that had taken hold of me. For when

I wrote those lines, I had congratulated myself on my originality in using Hobbes and Rousseau to symbolize these two contrasting views of human nature. It was clearly a case of unconscious plagiarism (thankfully I had never published it), but it nevertheless seemed incredible that I should have forgotten I got the idea from Pinker. For I had not just read his book; I had reviewed it for the *Evening Standard*, a London newspaper.

Perhaps my mind needed to forget the source of the idea, given that I had come to such a different conclusion. Whatever the reason, rereading the first few chapters of Pinker's book brought home to me the extent to which my thinking had been distorted prior to the Utopia Experiment. Some powerful psychological force had pushed it off track, to the extent of blanking out any countervailing facts or memories. Before I started thinking about doing the experiment, I had scoffed at romantic notions of noble savages, but by the time I headed up to Scotland my thoughts had done a 180-degree turn, and I had become a fervent primitivist. I longed to live in natural surroundings, and believed that all my worries and anxieties would vanish once I had left the trappings of civilization behind me.

How foolish I now felt! How naive and ridiculous! What was it that made me turn so completely against the technology I had previously embraced with a passion? What was it that transformed me into such a stereotypical Romantic, despite everything I had read beforehand about the realities of hunter-gatherer life? I struggled to put my finger on the moment when I had performed my intellectual volte-face, but I couldn't isolate a single event, a Road to Damascus experience that flipped me round all of a sudden. The more I thought about it, the more it seemed like a slow process, so slow in fact that I hadn't even noticed it.

Another piece of writing that seemed uncannily relevant, as if destiny had placed it there to chastise me, was something I found on Nick Bostrom's webpage.

Using the Internet was not easy in hospital. There was one computer, an old desktop machine, perched on a small table in the cramped office of someone whose function I never quite managed to figure out. He seemed to be some kind of community leader or youth-club manager, and he was only there for two hours each weekday. He would arrive at his office at midday, and from then until 2 pm a bunch of patients – the young ones in particular, but always the same crowd – would hang out there, eating jam doughnuts and crisps in some pale imitation of normality.

It wasn't until I had been in hospital for over a week that I discovered you could sign up for a twenty-minute slot on the computer in this bizarre hangout. The Internet connection was painfully slow, and my ability to compose emails was practically zero. Whenever I tried, the computer screen would start swimming in front of me, and my head would begin to feel all cloudy. I did, however, manage to do the occasional bit of browsing.

I was sitting there one day, aimlessly flicking through webpages that reminded me of my former life, when I thought of Nick Bostrom – who had introduced me to the Unabomber manifesto all those months ago – and wondered what he was up to. I went to his webpage, and there, near the top, were the following words, which seemed to speak directly to me, and sent a chill down my spine:

> What if I am overlooking something essential or getting a big thing wrong? Then whatever progress I'm making is in vain. It is worse than useless to travel fast and far if one is going in the wrong direction. How can one reduce the probability of such fundamental error? And of course, if one spends too much of one's time worrying about such questions, one never gets anywhere at all. In the ideal world, perhaps one would have two lives. In the first life, one would figure out what the right direction is. In the second life, one would set off in that direction at one's maximum pace.

It was as if Nick had anticipated my mistake. I had travelled as fast as I could along the path of my Utopia Experiment, and gone as far as I could, only to realize I was going in the wrong direction. And all that progress I had made was now therefore in vain. I had overlooked many essential things, and got more than one big thing wrong. And now I was spending my time worrying about it all, and going nowhere. I wished desperately that I could have another life, or at least go back in time to that moment when the idea for the experiment had first occurred to me, so I could crush it there and then, and set off in a different direction.

And I wondered how Nick could be so wise, and why I had made such a crazy blunder. We were both interested in the possibility of global collapse, but he was pursuing his research calmly and rationally, in the context of a renowned academic institution, whereas I had set up a badly organized camp in the freezing north of Scotland. Sure, there were some apparently sensible reasons for doing what I did, such as my desire to challenge myself and escape from what I increasingly felt to be a staid, bourgeois existence. But even these motives now appeared somewhat suspect.

Why had I been so dissatisfied with my life anyway? To many people, it would have seemed pretty good. I had had a great job, a lovely old house in the country, a beautiful girlfriend and a decent income. But I had grown sick of all these things, and it showed in an article I wrote for the *Guardian* in October 2005, entitled 'The loss of utopia':

> Look at the way we live now, in the west. We grow up in increasingly fragmented communities, hardly speaking to the people next door, and drive to work in our self-contained cars. We work in standardized offices and stop at the supermarket on our way home to buy production-line food which we eat without

relish. There is no great misery, no hunger, and no war. But nor is there great passion or joy. Despite our historically unprecedented wealth, more people than ever before suffer from depression.

Once again, the article said more about me than it did about the world. Perhaps I was already sliding into a depression back then, and the Utopia Experiment was a last desperate attempt to claw my way back out of the hole. Or perhaps I was just a spoilt kid, throwing his toys out of the pram in a fit of pique. Now I wanted them back, and I was stunned that I couldn't get them. There was no cosmic mama to make it all right again.

In his little-known but remarkably perceptive 1925 paper entitled 'Those Wrecked By Success', Freud wrote that 'people occasionally fall ill precisely when a deeply-rooted and long-cherished wish has come to fulfilment'. It seems, he added, 'as though they were not able to tolerate their happiness; for there can be no question that there is a causal connection between their success and their falling ill.' Maybe the Utopia Experiment was a deliberate, though unconscious, act of self-sabotage. Misery can be an art form, especially when there are no civil wars raging in your streets, no natural disasters, no mass starvation or pandemic striking down those around you.

Or maybe there was no deep Freudian explanation. Maybe I was simply bored. 'Boredom in the midst of paradise generated our first ancestor's appetite for the abyss,' wrote the philosopher E. M. Cioran. Maybe I just needed the lure of disaster to spice things up a bit.

It is often said that you don't learn the value of what you have until you lose it. Now, at least, I was determined not to take things for granted ever again.

When I first got to hospital, my physical condition was not much better than my mental state. Far from turning me into a horny-handed son of toil, my life in Utopia had weakened me, and left me gaunt and thin. Now I was eating normally, and I was beginning to put some weight back on. But I was still very weak, so the nurses encouraged me to use the hospital gym.

I started going every morning after breakfast, motivated in part by the presence of a pretty young gym instructor. I would start with ten minutes on the exercise bike or the treadmill, and then move on to some of the machines for building muscle strength. As I pulled down, slowly and painfully, on the metal bar above my head, or struggled to push back a vinyl pad with the soles of my feet, I would sometimes reflect on the irony of it all. Here I was, using a bunch of artificial contraptions to help restore the strength that a supposedly natural life outdoors had sapped. Looking back on how I had felt a year before, as I was preparing to quit my job and head up to Scotland, I recalled my feelings of being a caged animal, desperate to break free and return to the wild. Now I was back in the safety of the zoo, chastened to learn that I could not survive outside it.

Similar thoughts ran through my head when I attended a cooking lesson one afternoon. Three of us assembled in a room that seemed to have been built specially for the purpose, with three ovens and identical sets of bowls, wooden spoons, scales and pans. There was Terry, the middle-aged man I had met on my first morning in hospital, whose wife had supposedly got him locked up just so she didn't have to share a hotel room with him. There was Alex, a young man still in his teens who had arrived a few days after me, and who had been placed on suicide watch for his first night. And then there was me.

'Right!' said the matronly lady who had come to teach us. 'What would you like to cook today? How about cake? Shall we bake some little cakes?'

She spoke as if we were children, but it didn't annoy me in the slightest. On the contrary, it felt comforting, and slightly comical.

We all agreed that baking cakes was an excellent idea, and we proceeded to cream butter and sugar together, beat in some eggs, and fold in some flour, as instructed by our new surrogate mother. We spooned the mixture into the little paper cases and popped them in the oven. Ten minutes later, we all proudly removed our golden brown fairy cakes and set them aside to cool down.

How easy it all was, in this nice clean kitchen! How wonderful to be able to simply flick a switch and have a warm oven just a few minutes later! It had always been such an effort to get the Rayburn going, arranging the kindling properly so the fire would catch more easily, adding larger pieces of wood one by one so as not to put it out, and then waiting and waiting while the heavy cast-iron beast warmed up as slowly as a lizard straining for the first rays of sunlight. Was life really better that way? It had been easy to fantasize about the joys of simple living back home in the Cotswolds before heading up to Scotland, but it now seemed such a waste of precious time and brainpower. Yes, it could be meditative to do everything slowly, but was it necessary to do so every day? Couldn't my brain be doing more interesting things, thinking more interesting thoughts, if it wasn't focused on heating the oven?

10. SPRING

In March, the ranks of our fledgling community began to swell with the arrival of new volunteers. There was Nick Stenning, an eighteen-year-old who had just finished school and was taking a gap year before going to Cambridge University. Tall, with tousled red hair and pale blue eyes, he was as happy scything grass and chopping wood as discussing cosmology and playing the clarinet.

There was David Ross, the former Royal Marine, who now ran a small business making boots. He was in his fifties, but still hardy and with a soldier's can-do attitude. He was an invaluable companion on my regular scavenging trips to look for pieces of wood, scrap metal, and any other waste that could be used as building materials.

And there was Harmony, who played the flute, of course, and offered to perform music for inspiration and meditation. She was twenty-three but she looked even younger, her baby face flanked by long straight brown hair that fell messily around her shoulders. She was quiet, with a slightly melancholy air about her, but completely unfazed at being the only woman on site when she arrived.

Our growing numbers meant we had to take a more formal approach to decision-making, so I suggested we have a meeting each evening to decide what jobs needed doing the next day and to allocate tasks. Everyone seemed happy with this proposal, except Adam.

One evening, I got back to the Barn after a long day chopping wood, carrying water and sowing seeds. Agric was preparing vegetables on the large wooden table, while David lit the fire in the Rayburn. Adam was in his easy chair half asleep (though he was pretending to read a book), while Harmony sat nearby plucking softly at her guitar.

I cleared my throat, trying to call attention to what I was about to say, but no one looked up. I clapped my hands, and Adam roused himself from his slumber.

'OK, guys, let's try and figure out what we're all going to do tomorrow,' I said, trying to sound as cheerful and enthusiastic as possible.

'I'll chop some more wood, and do some digging,' said Nick.

'What about you, Adam?' I asked tentatively.

He snorted. 'Every last power of one over the other must go!' he proclaimed regally. 'If you see a job that needs doing, just do it yourself. Don't expect others to do it for you, or tell anyone else what to do. You can ask for help if you need it, and if they are moved by the Great Spirit to help then they will. But no orders!'

'That's just not practical, Adam,' I said, trying to remain calm. 'What about the jobs that nobody wants to do, like carrying water up from the stream, or washing up?'

'Everything is perfect,' beamed Adam. 'If nobody wants to do it, it's not meant to be.'

I took a deep breath, trying to work out how to shift this immovable object, but Agric seized the opportunity to explain the next steps in his master plan to grow enough food to keep us all fed throughout the next winter.

'We'll need a supply of dried beans,' he began. 'Currently we have a borlotto, which we are growing mostly for dried beans but which we can also use for pods early on. We also have a Blue Lake white-seeded pole bean, which is mostly for pods, but also has some dried-bean-worthiness. But we need more varieties that produce beans for drying. My preference is for climbing beans since they produce more per space, but we should grow one or more dwarf beans for drying, just to compare.'

I had no idea what all this meant, but I nodded my head sagely. 'If this experiment succeeds,' I thought to myself, 'it will be in large part thanks to Agric.'

Harmony raised her hand. 'I'm happy to do some sowing tomorrow morning,' she said. 'But I'd like to continue weaving my mattress on the peg loom in the afternoon.'

The loom was simply a row of wooden pegs fitted into a timber base. Each peg had a hole in the bottom through which string was threaded, so that tufts of un-spun fleece could be woven around the string. Harmony had mastered the knack quickly, but I was still struggling, despite Adam's several attempts to teach me. I would watch with a growing sense of incompetence as he took chunks of wool and teased them through his fingers, before weaving them in and out of the pegs, back and forth.

'I'll help you with the platform for the big yurt,' said David.

In addition to the two little yurts that Adam had made, we also had the pieces for a much bigger yurt that could sleep up to eight people. It was the genuine article – made in Mongolia and imported by an eccentric couple who bred alpacas in Wales. I had bought it from them just before coming to Scotland, and paid someone an exorbitant amount to drive it up here all the way from Wales in a small van. It had lain in its various pieces in the Barn for many months, waiting for the time when we had enough people to assemble it.

But before we could put it up, we had to build a platform for it, as I had for the little yurts the previous summer. We had already built a hexagonal framework of beams, and several of the six removable triangular sections of flooring that would be fastened to the beams. These sections were made of old plywood that someone in the nearest village had thrown away, with a layer of beech on top (reclaimed from someone's floor). Now we had to finish building the remaining sections, and coat them underneath with sump oil, and varnish the beech with Danish oil.

Despite Adam's stubborn insistence on doing things his own way, Utopia was beginning to feel like a real community. Not only were there more of us now, but we were all working together towards a common goal. Even Adam said he was committed to making the experiment a success, and he would often surprise me with a new talent or piece of handiwork. He built a wooden compost toilet, raised like a throne above a deep hole in the ground, single-handedly, though he never used it himself, preferring to shit *au naturel* and bury each turd in a new hole he would dig wherever he happened to deposit his droppings. He wove several thick fleece rugs on the peg loom that made passable mattresses to sleep on, though they were rather smelly and oily. One moment he would be talking very sensibly about how to make felt, or where to put the compost toilet, and the next he would be trying to figure out what the pigs were trying to tell us by digging a hole in a certain place, or describing his sacred duties as a high priest of the order of Melchizedek. I found him by turns frustrating and lovable, but always fascinating.

Not long after he arrived, Nick cut his finger with an axe while he was chopping wood. A friend of Romay's drove him to the nearest hospital. Thankfully it wasn't serious, and he only needed a few stitches. But without antiseptics and other simple elements of modern medicine that most of us take for granted, even minor injuries can be fatal. Small cuts can become infected, leading to a painful death from blood poisoning.

To be really authentic, I suppose we shouldn't have taken Nick to hospital. We should have just patched him up with whatever we had lying around. But what if his wound had gone bad? What if he had developed septicaemia, and become gravely ill? What if he had chopped his whole finger off?

From then on, I became terrified that one of the volunteers might get seriously hurt, or even killed. I took out third-party liability insurance, but that felt like cheating, like I wasn't fully embracing the radical uncertainty of primitive living. I had a foot in both worlds – one in the post-apocalyptic world where death stalks you at every turn, and the other in the risk-averse, overprotective world of modern Britain, where doctors wait in high-tech hospitals to kiss us better if we have the merest scratch. I hated having to make these compromises, and wished I could plunge wholeheartedly into the experiment, cutting all my ties to the world outside.

But did I really? Or was I secretly glad that civilization still existed out there, intact and ready to help out in times of emergency? I hated that thought most of all.

Nick's wounded finger meant he had to limit himself mainly to cooking and making things for the Barn (he rigged up a clothes line, that hung across the ceiling above the Rayburn, for example), and leave the more strenuous work to David and myself. David was indefatigable, always cheerful and ready to help out with any task at hand, from constructing the remaining flooring for the big yurt, to digging the vegetable patch. The only time I ever saw David lose his cool was one morning when Adam had decided to take a long lie-in.

'I know it's not the marines, but we need to have some modicum of discipline around here if we're going to get anything done,' he complained to me over a mug of tea. 'Adam isn't pulling his weight.'

'He did build that compost toilet,' I countered weakly.

'Yes, but right now we don't need a bloody throne,' said David. 'We need to get this platform finished so we can put up the big yurt. We need more sleeping space.'

'I know, but I've given up trying to tell Adam what to do. The only person Adam listens to is the Great Spirit.'

David shook his head.

'Fuck the Great Spirit,' he said.

A few days later, my friend Angus arrived. We had known each other since we were teenagers, and even though I only saw him once every one or two years, it always felt as if barely a day had passed since our previous meeting. Now he was just back from a two-year stint in Mexico and Guatemala, and was full of tales about shamans and ancient Maya rituals. His face bore the marks of a man who had lived; his skin was rough and his cheekbones looked chiselled by the wind, but his dark brown eyes always twinkled underneath his bushy eyebrows and wavy hair.

Angus could turn his hand to anything, and I doubt if we could have finished putting up the big yurt without him. Even with his help it took us almost a week. One reason it took so long was that this platform also turned out to be a little too small. At first we tried tightening the tension band to pull the lattice walls into a narrower cylinder, but this just pushed the roof poles up into the wrong angle, and we grudgingly accepted that we would have to make the platform bigger. It took two days to accomplish just this, since we had to coat the added pieces with sump oil underneath and varnish on top, as we had done for the original platform.

Dressing the yurt was a whole new task in itself. Fixing the rectangular sheep-wool felt segments to the lattice walls turned out to be more difficult than I had anticipated. They were heavy and unwieldy, and it took two or three people just to handle one segment. Fitting the two semi-circular felt covers to the roof was even harder, and required even more hands. Finally, the canvas outer layer proved to be the most challenging task of all. We all stood round the yurt, grabbing on to the outer edge of the huge tarpaulin, pulling and yielding in turn, but each time it looked just right to one person, someone else on the other side of the yurt would complain that it hung too far down on their side, or didn't hang down far enough. It was infuriating, and before long my arms were aching and my back was sore.

Angus ran round and round the yurt like a madman, telling one person to pull here, another to let go there.

Finally he yelled a big whoop of victory, and we all stood back to admire our work. She did look pretty impressive. Gertrude, as Adam insisted on calling her, cut a strange figure against the Scottish scenery. From a distance, it looked as though a big white spaceship had landed in a muddy field, a pristine and alien technology surrounded by bare-branched trees and, further away, snow-covered mountains.

On 1 April we held an open day and invited people from the nearest village to come and visit the site. Perhaps my choice of this particular date revealed greater ambivalence about the experiment than I was at that point willing to admit. Perhaps I was afraid of being taken too seriously.

I did, in fact, worry that dozens of people might come from all around the Highlands, since several Scottish newspapers had recently featured the experiment in prominent articles. It was headline news, no less, in the *Ross-shire Journal*, with a full-colour photo on the front page. The *Press and Journal* had also run a story a few days before.

As it was, only four or five visitors turned up: a middle-aged couple dressed in their Sunday best, a local farmer or two, a jolly housewife. There, in the middle of our shabby patch of ground, stood a white Mongolian yurt, with fine views over the Moray Firth and the mountains beyond. And inside the yurt, sitting cross-legged with their backs against the circular wall, were the volunteers, looking like they had just raided a thrift shop. Adam, with his bird's nest beard and leather breeches; Harmony, with her flute and woollen Nepalese cap; Agric, with his shock of white hair and hobnail boots. Unsurprisingly, the visitors looked rather bemused by the whole set-up.

I gestured for the visitors to sit down with the volunteers, and said a few words about the experiment. I explained that we weren't survivalists, that we didn't really think civilization was about to collapse, and that we were simply trying to imagine what life would be like if it did. The purpose, I said, was to raise awareness about global warming and peak oil, so we could do something to address these problems before it was too late. The visitors looked even more perplexed than before.

Then Adam and Harmony played some music, Adam plucking away at his guitar while Harmony accompanied him on the flute. Finally, Agric gave a little talk of his own, which didn't seem to make the visitors any less bewildered.

As I looked around at their faces, trying to work out what on earth they made of this experiment going on in their vicinity, I became increasingly agitated. Their puzzled expressions made me see, for perhaps the first time, how odd everything I was doing must have looked to the outside world. My friends and family had of course raised many objections when I told them about my plans over a year before, but I had brushed them off without a second thought. And since arriving in Scotland, I had lived in a world of my own creation, surrounded by people who believed in the project, and only venturing occasionally into civilization. Now, I was forcibly reminded of how bizarre the whole experiment must have looked to a casual stranger.

I could feel my heart beating faster and faster. I couldn't breathe. I needed to get out of the yurt and be alone. I longed for Agric to finish his talk.

But Agric showed no signs of wrapping up, and soon I couldn't stand it any longer. I got up, made my excuses, and ran down to the area beside the river where the two smaller yurts stood. I took refuge in one of them, curled up on the wooden floor in a foetal position, pulling whatever blankets and coverings I could find on top of me, and closed my eyes.

I don't know how long I stayed like that. But at some point, Scott peered in through the doorway, and asked me if I was all right.

Scott was in his fifties, and had lived in the Highlands for the past thirty years with his wife Jules. Short and wiry, with curly dark hair and piercing blue eyes, he was as tough as the granite peaks that overlooked his game-keeper's lodge. I had met him and Jules on my first trip to the Highlands, with Romay, in 1988, and had made a special point of seeing them on every visit since.

I shook my head. 'It's beginning to dawn on me how much I've taken on,' I said.

'Well, nobody said it was going to be a walk in the park,' said Scott. 'Look, you've been working flat out the past few weeks. You're probably just exhausted. Why don't you come back with us and rest for a day or two?'

I didn't need much persuading. Scott and Jules lived in a remote glen that made Utopia seem almost suburban by comparison. Even when you turned off the small winding road through the gates of the estate, it took another half hour to drive down the path to their cottage. It was surrounded by mountains on all sides, so they couldn't even get a TV signal. It would, in fact, have made a much better location for the experiment.

But in a way, Scott and Jules had been doing their own Utopia Experiment for the past few decades. They grew much of their own food and kept chickens. Scott chopped wood for the Rayburn every day, which cooked their food and heated their water. And Julia tended to magnificent vegetable patches that put our amateurish efforts to shame.

When we got back to their cottage that evening, Scott ran me a warm bath. The water in the back boiler on the Rayburn would get so hot that they had to run baths quite often just to stop it from exploding. As I lay there in the steaming tub, enjoying the first bath I had taken for many months, I could feel the tension in my muscles dissolve and the mental darkness dissipate. Later, the three of us ate thick lentil soup in their living room while the Rayburn blazed away and Scott sprinkled the conversation with nuggets of Highland folklore. That night, I slept more soundly than I had done for a long time.

The next morning Scott invited me to go for a walk with him. The light was faint and eerie, and the mist was still rising as we strolled down through the glen, each lost in our own thoughts. We reached a small stream that swirled chaotically around light grey rocks, and I crouched down beside it, mesmerized by the whirling water.

And there I stayed, gazing into the stream. It felt like hours, but it may have been less than a minute. Everything else faded from my vision, and all I could see were the eddies where the current tumbled around the rocks, and the only sound I could hear was the rush of the water. It seemed like the stream was whispering to me, inviting me into the vortex, and its voice was sweet and haunting and irresistible. I wished it would pull me into its frothy arms, and hold me in its cold, loving embrace for ever.

'Dylan, don't look at the water!'

Scott gripped my shoulder and pulled me back from the stream. His face was white. Somehow, he had sensed the danger, and broken the spell. He squinted into my eyes like a doctor looking for signs of life in a coma victim.

'Be careful,' he said. 'It's dangerous to look at the

stream for too long when you're in that frame of mind. The water can play strange tricks on you.'

I felt stunned. What had happened? Why did I get hypnotized by the stream? How did Scott know? Was it really dangerous?

I trusted Scott. He knew the glen intimately, every nook and cranny, and all the spirits that dwelt there. I felt sad to leave the stream behind me, but something told me Scott was right to drag me away.

When I got back to Utopia the following day, everyone was hard at work digging and planting. Harmony had left, and another female volunteer who had arrived had decided she couldn't face the primitive living conditions, and had gone straight back home the same day. Nick and David were nearing the end of their stay too, their places soon to be filled by Tommy and Pete, two twenty-one-year-old students at Newcastle University. Pete, from Belfast, was studying English, and Tommy, from nearby Holywood in County Down, was studying fine art. I had met them there several months before, when I had given a talk about the experiment in Newcastle.

Tommy was tall, with light red hair and pale blue eyes, and looked like he could handle himself in a fight. Pete was slightly smaller, with short dark hair, and more cerebral. They explained to me, in thick Belfast accents, why they had decided to volunteer.

'I'm here because I don't want to live in fear of not

being able to cope if society collapses,' said Pete. He thought that by learning to grow vegetables, look after pigs, weave fleece blankets and acquiring other pre-industrial skills, he'd be better prepared when civilization imploded.

'I'm also worried about a collapse,' said Tommy. Besides learning survival skills, he wanted to develop a visual culture for the project. That pleased me. I wanted the experiment to be as much about art and culture as about bodily survival. Right now, though, the priority was digging and planting the vegetable garden.

Tommy and Pete plunged into daily life at Utopia with enthusiasm. Agric found a willing student in Pete, who would listen attentively while he explained his schedule for sowing seeds, or his latest speculations on the date of the impending apocalypse. Tommy threw his back into digging the vegetable patch, and began work on a sign to welcome visitors. He was a graffiti artist and had brought some spray paint with him, so we found a large piece of plywood and Tommy proceeded to spell out UTOPIA in big, bright, bold letters, old school style, and we fixed up the sign to the side of the Barn. It looked rather incongruous, this splash of urban culture in the middle of the Scottish countryside, but no more so than the Mongolian yurt that stood nearby, or the throne-like compost toilet that Adam had built.

After they had been there about a week, I asked Pete and Tommy what they missed most about life back home.

'Music on demand,' said Pete, without hesitation.

Tommy nodded in agreement. 'I can't believe how much I miss my iPod!'

It's funny how quickly people become accustomed to something so radically new. For most of human history and all our prehistory the only music we could hear was the stuff we played ourselves. Then, in the last few thousand years, the very rich and powerful had the luxury of paid musicians to entertain them. Yet now, anyone can use technology to summon up a whole orchestra or a rock band. It's something many people take for granted, and think about only when for some odd reason – such as taking part in an experiment in post-apocalyptic living – they are deprived of it.

I certainly missed music too. I was used to listening to flawless recordings of the finest classical orchestras. Now the best I could get was Adam strumming his guitar and warbling away like a country and western singer with throat cancer. I wondered out loud whether, in the post-industrial future that we were trying to simulate, people might carefully preserve old iPods as valuable treasures. Tommy, an experienced dumpster-diver who used rubbish in his streetwise art, scoffed at the idea. 'There'll be thousands of the things lying around,' he said. 'You'll just have to wander into the abandoned houses and pick them up.'

'Sure, but how long will they be usable?' I asked. 'Their batteries will soon run out, and then what? Even if we manage to keep charging things for a while with solar panels or generators, they will eventually break down, and then everything electronic will soon become unusable.'

'Great!' interjected Adam. 'I hate canned music.'

It is one thing to live without technology that you have never experienced, and quite another to go without it after you have enjoyed it. Our hunter-gatherer ancestors didn't miss iPods, but I sure did in Utopia.

I began to wonder whether these feelings might point to a weakness in the primitivist credo. Even if the nomadic lifestyle before the advent of agriculture really was better, or more authentic, or more whatever, than the sedentary existence that followed it, we can't simply return to it now, as if the intervening ten thousand years never happened. Primitivists admit this much, and argue that we will need a process of 'rewilding' to readjust to our natural state, but they don't seem to realize that this would take generations, not years. If civilization collapsed, and we didn't rebuild it, then perhaps after a few centuries people might recover the lost innocence of the original hunter-gatherers, but the first or second generation of survivors certainly wouldn't. The memories of civilization could not simply be erased; they would gnaw at the survivors, and torture them with the recollection of comforts never again to be enjoyed.

An animal born in captivity does not suddenly revert to a wild state if released back into the jungle. On the contrary, it is shell-shocked, and lost.

*

Besides discussing the things we missed, or didn't miss, about civilization, we also occasionally argued about what life would be like long after civilization had collapsed – not the first few years after the crash, which we were attempting to simulate, but a hundred years later, or a thousand.

One possibility was that we would end up in a situation like that described by Ernest Callenbach in his short story 'Chocco'. The narrator is the thirty-first Memory Keeper of the Sun People. He tells the story of a long-lost civilization called the Machine People. It soon becomes clear that the Machine People are us – citizens of the twenty-first century – and that little now remains of our industrial civilization except networks of empty roads and the rusting hulks of millions of cars. The Sun People are our distant descendants, who have returned to the nomadic ways of our hunter-gatherer ancestors, but preserve the memory of the Machine People as a warning of how things can go terribly wrong. As the story proceeds, we learn that the world of the Machine People collapsed due to rampant pollution, climate change, and a shortage of fossil fuels. The Sun People are descended from a few rebels who rejected the greed and materialism of the Machine People, smoked marijuana, grew their hair long and worshipped Gaia – a bunch of hippies, in other words. The Sun People are determined not to repeat the errors of their industrial forebears, by, for example, reinventing complex technology.

Nick Bostrom calls this kind of scenario, in which our

current economic and technological capabilities are lost and never rebuilt, *unrecovered collapse*. He argues that this is unlikely, since it is hard to think of a good reason why recovery would *not* occur. It seems part of human nature to innovate, and all it takes is for one person, or one group, to get a technological edge, and others will be compelled to adopt it or perish. Only if some critical resource were permanently exhausted or destroyed, or the human gene pool irreversibly degenerated, or some discovery were made that enabled tiny groups to bring down civilization at will, might humans fail to recover from a global collapse and remain forever at some pre-industrial level.

The alternative possibility is that, following a global catastrophe, the survivors start to rebuild civilization, with the result that sooner or later we end up back where we are today, as in *The Postman*, a 1997 film starring Kevin Costner. Based on David Brin's 1985 novel of the same name, it tells the story of a wandering survivor (Costner) who finds a dead postman and a bag of mail. Donning the dead man's uniform and taking the mailbag, he stumbles across a settlement, where he pretends to be a real postman from the newly restored government. Gradually, his lie takes on a life of its own as he inducts more volunteers into the fictional postal service. The volunteers carry letters between settlements and inadvertently spread the myth of the restored government. In the final scene of the movie, a crowd of people is gathered to witness the unveiling of a statue of the protagonist, who is recently deceased. From their modern clothing, and signs of contemporary technology, it is clear that civilization has been rebuilt, and is now back to its pre-apocalyptic status.

This is meant to be an optimistic scenario, but to those of us at Utopia it was deeply depressing. Would humanity learn nothing from a global collapse, and repeat the same mistakes that led to disaster in the first place? And if so, what would happen next? Would there be a never-ending cycle of collapse and rebirth? Would the human race be condemned to some kind of Nietzschean eternal return of the same, as in the *Ragnarök* of Norse mythology, in which the world is consumed by flames, only to resurface anew and be repopulated by the survivors, thus starting the whole tragedy all over again?

It was clear which of these two scenarios we preferred. Permanent primitivism was our idea of Utopia. And we preferred not to ask ourselves how plausible this really was.

A third possibility, which we never discussed, is that civilization might not keep on collapsing and re-emerging over and over again, but that at some point would reach escape velocity, and attain a vastly superior level of technological sophistication than that which we currently enjoy. In this scenario, our descendants construct advanced artificial intelligence, enhance their bodies by means of molecular nanotechnology, and colonize the rest of our galaxy.

This was the scenario that the Unabomber feared,

because he was convinced that such far-reaching technological development would reduce humans to mere cogs in a huge impersonal machine. But what if he was wrong? What if there are long-term technological futures in which life is better than it is today? Science fiction has little to offer the imagination here. Dystopian plots far outnumber the few utopian ones. Robots turn against us (*I, Robot*), telescreens are used to brainwash us and monitor our every move (*1984*), or – even worse – historical memory, art and literature, religion and philosophy, are all purged in the name of pleasure and order (*Brave New World*). The few positive visions seem to be aimed at children, like *The Jetsons*, an American cartoon from the 1960s, and Tomorrowland, one of the areas in Disneyland. 'Tomorrow can be a wonderful age,' Walt Disney himself insisted. 'Our scientists today are opening the doors of the Space Age to achievements that will benefit our children and generations to come. The Tomorrowland attractions have been designed to give you an opportunity to participate in adventures that are a living blueprint of our future.' That kind of optimism about the future seems rather quaint now.

Why are we so bad at imagining positive forms of technological change? Is it due to some innate conservative bias etched deeply into human nature, or merely a contingent feature of contemporary society? Francis Bacon was able to imagine all sorts of wonderful technological developments in his seventeenth-century Utopia, *New Atlantis*. Humans would breed plants to grow bigger and produce sweeter fruit, design machines for controlling the weather, and build skyscrapers half a mile high. Such optimism seems alien in today's cynical world, but it seems perverse to rule out the possibility of a bright future in which technology leads to a net improvement in the human condition.

If pressed, most of us will admit that there's something profoundly unknowable about the future, especially a distant future, and yet we still feel hunches about the way things are heading. These hunches reveal more about our personal temperament – our individual proclivities towards optimism or pessimism – than about the world itself.

As time wound on, our conversations in Utopia began to take on a darker hue. In particular, as we continued to speculate about life after the crash, the subject of violence would crop up with increasing frequency.

Several of the volunteers had already raised doubts about the scenario I had sketched out as a framework for the experiment, which portrayed our settlement as a group of strangers who had seen the writing on the wall and had come together to prepare for the impending collapse of civilization. By the time disaster struck, they would be in an enviable position; located far from the chaos of the big cities, with their own supply of food and water, their camp would be a magnet for less well-prepared survivors. And not many newcomers could be accommodated. The land could only support a limited number of people. Sooner or later we would have to stop people from coming in. Would those unwelcome visitors simply turn round and go away? What if they were starving? What if there were lots of them? What if they were armed?

When the topic came up again one evening, Pete suggested we organize some exercises during the experiment in which we would simulate an attack on the community by marauding gunmen. But how would we defend ourselves? We hadn't stockpiled any guns ourselves, so we would have to make our own weapons.

'Personally I like the idea of utilizing booby traps,' mused Angus. 'This keeps us at a distance from a potential enemy and out of harm's way.'

'How about a couple of longbows trained on visitors as a deterrent?' suggested Pete.

Angus nodded in approval, but then paused for a moment. 'That could make intruders more determined to hit first, to gain the element of surprise. What about having a few big dogs around? Ferocious ones, with a great sense of smell and hearing!'

'Good idea,' said Tommy. 'And they would be good company to keep when hunting and foraging away from Utopia.'

'And what about organizing a few workshops in bomb-making?' Angus went on. 'A couple of petrol bombs should deter most thieves. Anyone have an interest in pyrotechnics, or any experience with mining or demolition?'

Nobody raised their hand.

'We'd better read up on this shit then,' said Angus.

The conversation about defence was all well and good as an exercise in collaborative fiction, but as time went on I began to get worried that it was acquiring an increasingly realistic tone. The subject seemed to exert a weird fascination on the group, like a flame around which we bedraggled moths began to circle ever more closely. New solutions to the problem would be suggested, but the conversation always seemed to end with what became Angus's most memorable stock-phrase: 'Attack dogs and pipe bombs'.

One evening, as we returned once again to the topic, I caught sight of one of the volunteers take out a big hunting knife and caress the blade lovingly with his index finger. A copy of the Unabomber manifesto lay open on the table. If a police officer happened to come in now, I thought to myself, he might easily mistake us for some rabid bunch of eco-terrorists, holed up in the woods and preparing for their next atrocity.

As if he had caught my thought, Adam leapt to his feet.

'Can you hear that?' he hissed.

'What?'

'It's a helicopter! Come outside!'

Reluctantly, and slightly fearfully, I followed Adam out of the Barn. It was dark outside, and I couldn't see anything in the cloudy sky, but the sound, though faint, was unmistakable. It was the dull thud-thud-thud of helicopter blades.

'I told you they were watching us,' whispered Adam.

The more we discussed the likelihood of violence in the post-apocalyptic world, and the need for defence, the gloomier I became about the prospects for the kind of utopian world I'd imagined in my original scenario. That story was a typical example of what the science fiction writer Brian Aldiss once referred to, dismissively, as a 'cosy catastrophe'. This scenario is perhaps best exemplified by *News from Nowhere*, a novel by William Morris, in which the protagonist falls asleep in late Victorian England, and awakes to find himself in the year 2102. The industrial squalor he knows has vanished, and London has become a collection of pretty villages where everyone lives in peace and equality. He learns that a bloody civil war in the mid-twentieth century culminated in the destruction of the Industrial Revolution's dark satanic mills, clearing the way for a more beautiful world to spring up in their wake.

The novel had entranced me when I first read it, as I was preparing to leave for Scotland, but now it seemed preposterous. I was beginning to think that Cormac McCarthy was a better guide to life after the crash than the starry-eyed Morris. The post-apocalyptic world evoked in McCarthy's novel *The Road* is unremittingly bleak. The land is covered with ash and devoid of plant and animal life. The few human survivors have resorted to cannibalism, roasting newborn infants and slowly harvesting the flesh from their prisoners. But why would one even want to survive in such a world? What keeps the father and his young son trudging southwards in that novel? The mother, who committed suicide soon after the unexplained cataclysm, was surely more rational.

There is no insurance policy against the collapse of civilization. Even in the most well-prepared survivalist camp, life after a global collapse would be a grim affair. I'm sure the high-end doomsday bunker built by Vivos under the grasslands of Nebraska is very comfortable, but the 950 people who have each paid the $25,000 reservation fee will have to come to the surface when their food supplies run out. And then they'll have to deal with the chaos like everyone else. So even if you think the apocalypse is imminent, you're probably better off not bothering to prepare, and just taking your chances with everybody else when the shit hits the fan.

11. ON THE EDGE

One day in early April, I got a letter from the Area Planning and Building Standards Manager at the Highland Council. 'During a recent visit,' it said, 'it became apparent that development has commenced prior to the granting of planning permission.' The letter also asked me to 'halt all works on site' until such permission was granted. 'Failure to do so,' it concluded, 'may result in formal enforcement action being taken against you.'

I couldn't recall anyone from the Highland Council paying a visit to Utopia, so I was rather perplexed. Perhaps one of the people attending the open day was a council official in disguise? Or perhaps word had simply found its way back to the council by means of the social grapevine that mysteriously connects everyone in the Highlands. But one way or another, the Planning and Building Standards Office was now involved.

Apparently I needed to apply for permission to put up the yurts, and to convert the Barn into a kitchen and dining area. This seemed bizarre to me, given that none of this was permanent, and we'd be taking everything away when the experiment came to an end next year. But that was the law, and I began to worry that officials might descend on Utopia at any time and shut the experiment down.

And so I began the lengthy process of applying for planning permission. This involved filling out numerous forms, taking photographs of the Barn, and producing scale drawings of the yurts and other structures we intended to build. The kitchen table in the Barn was always either being used to prepare food, or cluttered with tools, so I had to spend long hours in Romay's farmhouse, which increased my sense of isolation from the experiment.

Civilization was like quicksand. The more I struggled to break free from it, the more it sucked me back in, suffocating me with its rules and regulations. The irony of jumping through so many bureaucratic hoops in order to pursue an experiment in primitive living didn't escape me. But it didn't amuse me either. One of the biggest attractions about the experiment had been the promise of a life free from paperwork. And now I was drowning in it.

The paperwork only increased when we decided to build a reed bed sewage system to treat our wastewater. When it was just Adam, Agric and me on site, we had washed our dishes and our clothes in the stream, and occasionally scrubbed ourselves down in the old whisky barrel we had sawn in half. But now we had hot water in the Barn and there were more volunteers living at Utopia, and we didn't want to pollute our precious stream or ruin our land by throwing our grey water away just anywhere.

A reed bed is basically just a shallow pond filled with gravel of different sizes with reeds growing on the surface. The wastewater flows in at one end and gradually seeps through the reeds, which pull oxygen down into their roots to feed the aerobic microorganisms that purify the water. By the time the water flows out at the other end of the reed bed, it is clean enough to go right back into the environment.

But of course the Highland Council demanded evidence that the system would work, and an engineer's report that complied with the British Good Building Guide. And we would also need to carry out a percolation test, and submit the results to the Scottish Environmental Protection Agency (SEPA). This meant more forms – and more application fees.

At least we didn't need permission to build a compost toilet. Or at least, we thought we didn't, and I didn't check with the council for fear of adding to my bureaucratic burden. In addition to the makeshift toilet I had hacked together at the start, there was Adam's more grandiose construction, complete with a little roof and a set of wooden steps. The principle was the same in both: after each crap, you needed to grab a handful of sawdust from the pile we kept nearby and scatter it over the fresh turds. When the bucket was full, it would be used as compost.

It was, needless to say, quite smelly, and not everyone went to get more sawdust when it ran out, or emptied the bucket of shit when it was full. But worst of all, for these tender refugees from the modern world, was the lack of toilet paper. The Chinese were using paper to wipe their bottoms fifteen hundred years ago, but until the late nineteenth century everyone else just used their hands, apart from a few wealthy people who used wool, lace or hemp. Many people still use their hands in the developing world, but for those who have grown up in the affluent West, it doesn't come easy, so we would clean our bottoms with wood shavings, leaves, grass, moss, snow, ferns, or whatever else we could find lying around nearby.

Though it was he who had built the compost loo, Adam steadfastly refused to use it.

'Adam,' I said to him at supper one evening, 'you've got to start using the compost toilet.'

There was no reply, just the sound of slurping as he pushed spoonfuls of beans into the opening in his beard.

I decided to press my point home.

'If everyone did what you do, and dug a separate hole every time they had a shit, then by the end of the experiment the place would be covered in thousands of little mounds, each containing a single turd. Please could you shit in the bucket like everyone else!'

This was too much for Adam. He slammed his empty plate down on the table, and stomped out.

*

Adam began spending more time on his own, cultivating his heart-shaped herb garden down by the stream, and making little improvements to the yurts. Among the more useful things he made were several sets of shelves that could be hung from the lattice walls. They were simple but clever, consisting of nothing more than three small planks of wood with four lengths of nylon cord threaded through holes in each corner. Adam had tied several knots in each piece of cord so that when the contraption was suspended vertically, the planks rested on the knots, forming more or less horizontal shelves.

The shelves were a godsend. It is not until you have to live for some time with all your things scattered around on the floor that you realize quite how important it is to have a few raised surfaces. We didn't keep much stuff in our yurts – just clothes mainly, plus some wood for the stove, a few candles, some matches and a torch. But when the floor was covered in sleeping bags and blankets, it could be frustratingly difficult to locate your torch when you really needed it, which was generally in the middle of the night, when you were bursting to go for a pee. It's vital to have your light source ready to hand if you don't want to spend ten minutes groping about the dark, especially if there are two other people curled asleep, who will not appreciate it if your probing fingers mistake some part of their anatomy for the torch you are seeking. Having a few shelves on which to store such things made life much easier, and once again I was grateful to Adam for his skill and experience in yurt life.

Tommy was annoyed that Adam wasn't even pretending to muck in with everyone else any longer. He scoffed at the little herb garden that Adam mentioned whenever anyone accused him of not doing anything. 'Fuck herbs!' he roared at Adam on one such occasion. 'They're a luxury. We need to grow food! Food that we can eat!'

Angus, though, was quite happy that Adam was down at the herb garden. 'He's more of a hindrance when he's around,' he sighed. 'Good riddance, I say.'

I began to wonder if I would have been happier if I had done the experiment on my own, like Thoreau in his hut by Walden Pond, or the Unabomber in his log cabin in Montana. Far from being a solace, the community I had created had come to feel oppressive and claustrophobic. In my former life, in my little cottage in the Cotswolds, I spent lots of time alone, and now I missed those hours, those days – even weeks – of silent contemplation, of uninterrupted reading, of long solitary walks in the country. Now I was far away from civilization, in one of the least populated parts of Europe, and I couldn't get away from people. When Jean-Paul Sartre remarked that 'hell is other people', I doubt he had the Scottish Highlands in mind.

In the second week of April, a journalist from *The Times* came to stay with us for a week. He wanted to write a big article about the experiment, and, after discussing it with the volunteers, I agreed to let him visit.

Ross arrived in a taxi, with three chickens – cellophane-wrapped and oven-ready. 'I may spend the week cold, wet and useless,' he smiled, 'but I'm damned if I'll starve!'

There didn't seem much chance of that. Ross described himself as 'an overweight, fifty-four-year-old city boy with a serious good-food, Old Holborn and rum habit.' I showed him into the Barn and introduced him to Pete, who was busy kneading the dough for the next batch of bread, and Agric, who was instructing Pete on the finer points of bakery. Pete's eyes watered when he saw the chickens.

Linda was also there. Fresh out of school in her native Ecuador, she had come to the UK for a year to learn English, and was paying a visit to Utopia because, as she informed Ross, 'I have nothing better to do.' Then I led him past the big Mongolian yurt and down into the valley where the smaller yurts sat by the stream.

On the way down I introduced Ross to Angus, who was hard at work reconstructing the tiny, one-person wooden hut that he had built to house a new toilet. A gale had demolished it early that morning. Linda had been inside moments before, and had barely managed to haul up her jeans and run out before the wind tore it apart. Had she not taken decisive action when the flimsy structure started shaking and creaking around her, she would have been rather exposed. Angus had now rebuilt the thing and was weighting it down with ropes and breezeblocks.

I showed Ross his yurt, which he would be sharing with Pete. Ross seemed both impressed by Adam's craftsmanship and appalled by the primitive nature of his sleeping quarters. His normal minimum bedtime requirements, he informed me, included central-heating radiators on low, a firm but deep mattress, a 13-tog duvet, two fluffy pillows and a Cuban woman (his wife was from Cuba). 'But, hey: it's the end of the world,' he laughed, good-naturedly. 'I suppose a chap has to make sacrifices.'

Ross was still unpacking his rucksack when Agric came bustling down the slope and press-ganged him into digging the vegetable patch. The journalist was clearly unused to physical labour: after just ten minutes, beads of sweat were forming on his forehead and he was exhausted.

'Time for a nap,' he sighed, and trundled back down to his yurt.

The next day I asked Ross if I could have a word with him in private. He was an outsider, with a fresh pair of eyes and no personal stake in the experiment. I wanted to know how it all struck him, and whether he thought we were all nuts.

We retired to his yurt, and I sat cross-legged while Ross tried in vain to find a comfortable way of squatting on the hard floor. In his subsequent feature for *The Times*, Ross would write that I looked gaunt, tense and stressed.

'Have you got any advice for me?' I asked.

'Not really,' said Ross. 'I think you're doing pretty well.'

I squinted at him in disbelief. Was he saying this just to make me feel better?

'But we're nowhere near self-sufficient,' I said. 'And I'm getting really low on funds.'

'Relax,' said Ross, 'this is going to work.'

'Really?' I asked. 'You really think so?'

He nodded, and smiled. 'Just look after your health, OK?'

Just when we should have been focusing all our efforts on planting the summer crops, we embarked on the most quixotic endeavour of the whole experiment. Romay had persuaded me to purchase an old Victorian signal box that sat in some local's garden and which he no longer wanted. It was a small wooden building that once housed the mechanical levers for controlling the points and signals on the old railway line. Romay thought it would make an excellent place for drying out the felt we planned to make from the fleeces we had acquired, as well as being a suitably historic and characterful addition to the Utopia estate. But taking down the signal box and moving it to Utopia turned out to be a much bigger job than any of us had anticipated.

To start with, it was just a matter of one or two volunteers heading over to the garden where the signal box sat, and dismantling it piece by piece. But after the nails and superficial fittings were removed, it required more than just two people to remove the beams and wallposts, and the project came to absorb more and more of our labour, leading us to neglect more pressing jobs such as tending our vegetable patches and chopping wood. Even dismantled, the sections were too big to fit on the trailer I had rented to transport it to Utopia, so Angus had to saw bits off. As we brought the structure over to Utopia in bits and pieces, I felt like Fitzcarraldo, trying to pull a 320-ton steamship over a steep hill in the Amazon jungle. It was just as exhausting, and just as ridiculous.

Then, when all the bits and pieces were finally lying in stacks around Utopia, we started to reconstruct it. Even with the help of a master builder who lived nearby, it was fiendishly complicated, like an Ikea kit designed by a malevolent demon, but without any instructions. Eventually we had no choice but to return to the vegetable patches, or risk losing our summer crop altogether. And so we abandoned the signal box in its half-finished state, and there it stayed, incomplete, for the rest of the experiment, a constant reminder of my folly. The whole process had been a huge waste of time and energy, a pointless distraction from the real tasks of daily survival, and it left me exhausted and despondent. Gazing balefully at the battered structure, I sighed and looked at Angus. 'Sometimes you stick your toe in the water,' I said, 'and before you know it you've started a process that you can't extricate yourself from.'

The signal box also cost me far more than I had

anticipated. I couldn't ask the master builder to spend several days helping us for free, and the previous owners of the signal box were now insisting I pay for the pleasure of removing it from their garden. I had originally been under the impression that it was available free to anyone who would dismantle it and take it away, but the owner demanded several hundred pounds for it. 'This will have cost a grand by the time we're finished,' muttered Angus. 'We could have bought a brand new log cabin for that!'

I had made a tidy profit when I sold my house, and I had been using this money to fund the experiment. It didn't cost very much to buy the basic vegetables needed in the first few months before we were able to start eating our first crops, and even less to supplement these thereafter, but it all added up, and on top of that was the rent I was shelling out for Bo's cottage, and a hundred other little things like stoves for the yurts, and seeds for the crops, and spades and shovels and axes and fleeces and candles and planks and hammers and saws and all the other things we had apparently managed to salvage from the wreckage of civilization.

Nine months after arriving in Scotland, my money was fast running out. I wasn't even sure I would have enough to keep the experiment going for the whole eighteen months. Even if I did, there wouldn't be much left at the end. And then what?

Strange as it may seem, I had never really pondered this question before. Not once, since the idea for the experiment first occurred to me in Mexico, had I thought about what I would do after it was over. It wasn't as if I had planned to stay in Scotland forever. On the contrary, the Utopia Experiment had always been a time-limited project, with a definite end date. So the complete lack of any plan for what I would do afterwards was, in hindsight, quite puzzling.

Perhaps, deep down, I never thought I would survive it. Or perhaps I thought that civilization really would collapse while the experiment was still ongoing, and then there would be nothing for it but to stay there. Whatever the reason for my neglect, it couldn't last, and by spring 2007 my dwindling finances were beginning to intrude on my consciousness, and the question of what I would do when the experiment finished was starting to nag away, at first quietly, and then with increasing urgency.

Eventually, I confided in Agric.

'I'm getting a bit worried about money,' I said one day. 'What if I run out, and can't afford to keep buying food?'

'Don't worry,' Agric reassured me. 'We'll be completely self-sufficient soon. And anyway,' he added, with a twinkle in his eye, 'I think you'll find things will change substantially within a month or two.'

I was puzzled by this remark, but I didn't press Agric for an explanation. I was grateful for his vague expression of optimism, and for now that was enough. But over the following days, as I returned to the topic of money in other furtive conversations with him, I began to probe the mysterious source of his confidence. Did he, perhaps, believe that we would find some wealthy philanthropist who would fund the experiment when my money ran out? Would we be able to turn Utopia into a profitable enterprise when the experiment was over, by running courses in post-apocalyptic survival skills, for example, or in permaculture?

But as I eliminated each of these hypotheses in turn, it gradually dawned on me that Agric's confidence was inspired by nothing so banal as the appearance of another funding source. It was, in fact, driven by his overwhelming certainty that civilization would collapse that very year. 'The world turns,' he confided to me one evening, with a glint in his eye. 'Within six months I expect it to look significantly different from now. I don't think people will like it so much . . .' And then he quoted Shakespeare:

> 'By the pricking of my thumbs,
> Something wicked this way comes.'

Far from being consoling, Agric's certainty unnerved me, for I realized I did not share it. Although the estimate I'd given Nick – that I thought there was a 50 per cent chance that civilization would collapse in the next few years – had seemed ridiculously high to him, it was probably quite low by Agric's standards. For it meant that I believed there was still a 50 per cent chance that civilization would not collapse within the next few years.

And that, to Agric, would have seemed like overweening optimism.

One afternoon, I noticed some broken plates, a rusty horseshoe and a few pieces of cutlery lying around on the grass down by the river. It made me very angry to see such carelessness, such mess. The Utopia Experiment was supposed to be about living in harmony with nature, not polluting it like the industrial civilization that we had left behind. Were we just repeating the same mistakes, screwing up our environment like every other society in human history? Or was this yet another sign of my deepening depression, leading me to notice the slightest evidence of dirt and decay? I gathered together the pieces in a pile, and as I did I noticed more rubbish lying around under the platform of the cooking area we had built by the yurts.

There could only be one person responsible for this mess – Adam. I flung aside the canvas flap and peered inside his yurt. He wasn't there, but there was a pile of tools that had gone missing from the Barn, and some food that he had obviously squirrelled away for his own private consumption. I gathered up the tools and the food and stuffed everything in a wooden potato crate along with the cutlery and broken plates, and marched up to the Barn.

Half an hour later, Adam stormed in.

'Who cleared away my shrine?' he bellowed.

'What fucking shrine?' I shouted back. 'Do you mean

those broken plates you left lying around by the river? It was a mess!'

'It was perfect,' said Adam. 'You had no right to clear that away. If you can't see the beauty in it, that's your problem. Those pieces were just perfect the way they were.'

Adam was staking a claim to his part of Utopia. He had already hinted, on a number of occasions, that he expected the volunteers to split into two groups – a sinful group of meat-eaters, under my command, and a pure group of vegetarians, under Adam's spiritual guidance. The meat-eaters would live in the Barn, a straight-walled stone building, while the vegetarians would live down by the stream in the small round blue yurts. At first I had just dismissed these suggestions as flights of fancy, but as it became clear that Adam was serious, I realized I would have to confront him.

That night, I woke from my sleep to hear two voices whispering outside the yurt. I wasn't sure who it was, and I didn't catch all the words, but it was clear they were talking about Adam.

'He's stealing food from the Barn and hiding it in his yurt, for fuck's sake!'

'I know, and he keeps some of the tools down there too. I was looking for the saw yesterday and I couldn't find the bloody thing.'

'We should hold some kind of trial.'

'What would the punishment be, if we find him guilty?'

At that moment, the wind began to howl, and I didn't catch the whole reply, but I fancied I heard something about cutting off Adam's hands.

'We can't do that, you crazy fucker!'

'Why not? It's not as if the police exist any more is it?'

Again, the noise of the wind obscured the reply. But the last remark puzzled me. Did the mystery speaker simply mean that, in the fictional scenario we were acting out, there would be no police force? Or did he somehow believe that civilization had actually collapsed, and there really were no police any more? The second possibility seemed far-fetched, but some of the volunteers were beginning to take it all very seriously, and this wasn't the first time I had wondered whether the slim line between fantasy and reality might be fading away.

I should have known this was likely to happen. I had long been aware of the Stanford Prison Experiment, but some blind spot had prevented me from perceiving the obvious parallels with Utopia, and drawing some potentially illuminating lessons. In 1971 a psychology professor called Philip Zimbardo had created a mock prison in the basement of the Stanford psychology building. Twenty-four male students volunteered to live there for a couple of weeks, with half taking on the role of prisoners, and the other half the role of guards.

On the second day of the experiment some of the prisoners blockaded their cell door with their beds and refused to come out or follow the guards' instructions.

The guards then set up a privilege cell in which prisoners who were not involved in the riot were given better meals. But the privileged inmates chose not to eat the better meals as a gesture of solidarity with their less fortunate companions, and the conflict escalated. Soon, one prisoner began, as Zimbardo put it, 'to act crazy, to scream, to curse, to go into a rage that seemed out of control'.

The guards became increasingly cruel as the experiment went on. They placed buckets in the cells and wouldn't let the prisoners urinate or defecate anywhere else. They wouldn't let the prisoners empty the buckets, which filled up with faeces, and the cells began to smell. The guards would punish the prisoners by removing their mattresses, leaving them to sleep on the concrete floor. By the sixth day Zimbardo decided things had gone too far, and cut the experiment short.

It may once have been possible to interpret Zimbardo's experiment as revealing some kind of innate sadism, some evil that is intrinsic to human nature. But that interpretation seems to have been undermined by a later attempt to replicate the experiment. When the BBC re-created Zimbardo's set-up in 2002, the guards did not degenerate into sadistic tyrants, and some even felt guilty about having power over the prisoners.

The real meaning of the Stanford Prison Experiment is that people very easily identify with the roles they play. The actual behaviour that results from taking on a given role will depend on a whole variety of factors, but the role itself will soon feel natural. This is in fact no more than what Plato pointed out over two thousand years before Zimbardo, when he warned against the dangers of acting. 'Have you not noticed,' he wrote in *The Republic*, 'how dramatic representations, if indulgence in them is prolonged into adult life, establish habits of physical poise, intonation and thought which become second nature?' The face takes on the shape of the mask it wears. Indeed our word *personality* is derived from the Latin *persona*, which referred to a theatrical mask.

I should have known, then, that the volunteers would likely become captivated by the roles they were playing, that what started out as a simulation would eventually become somewhat more than that, and take on an air of increasing realism. But once again something that should have been obvious took me by surprise, and I only recalled the Stanford Prison Experiment when it was too late.

Over the course of the next two weeks, Adam kept threatening to leave Utopia and take one of the small yurts with him.

'It's not your yurt to take, Adam,' I said, on one such occasion. 'It belongs to the experiment. And it's not your experiment either.'

'I'm doing a different experiment,' he replied, changing tack. 'You can do yours up here, in the Barn area. I'll do mine down there, by the river. That will be Adam-land. I don't believe in all this stuff about civilization collapsing anyway. I just want to live in accordance with the wishes of the Great Spirit.'

'That's not going to happen. And unless you can join in properly, and stop messing everything up, you'll have to leave.'

'Don't worry,' Adam snarled. 'I already got your message. Clear out! That's what you were telling me when you removed my shrine. Don't worry, I'm going.'

Then he went back to his yurt and slept for the rest of the day.

The next day, he was gone.

I never saw Adam again. And though there was much less dissension in Utopia after he had gone, I came to miss him and his bizarre antics. And I realized that, of all the volunteers, I liked him the most. In fact, he was the only one for whom I really felt any affection at all – apart from Angus, who was an old friend, and technically not a 'volunteer' at all.

This made no sense. Adam could be disruptive, selfish and uncooperative. His constant references to the Great Spirit were transparently self-serving, and usually justified him taking a long nap while everyone else was working, or cultivating his heart-shaped herb garden instead of tending to staple crops.

But I found him fascinating. And more than that, there was something about him that resonated with me, something I felt drawn to. He was infuriating at times, but he could also be extremely funny, and very caring. And he was there right from the beginning, building the first yurts with me, cooking the first meals, chopping wood, when there was nobody else there, just the two of us.

I don't think anyone else felt like this about him. Perhaps they saw him more accurately. 'The ultimate paradox: a grumpy hippie,' Ross had remarked. Angus put it more bluntly: 'A fucking chancer,' he grumbled. Everybody else seemed relieved to get rid of him. But for me, Utopia wasn't quite so colourful without him. It began, in fact, to seem increasingly bleak.

12. SURVIVAL

In May, my growing doubts and fears finally coalesced into the biting, shattering conclusion that the whole experiment had been a huge mistake. I recall waking up one night, my heart beating rapidly, as if icy fingers were clawing at my chest. In the dim light I could just make out the shape of a bird's skull suspended on a thread from the ceiling, twisting gently in the breeze from a crack in the canvas. The smell of damp socks mingled with the odour of stale wood smoke. On the other side of the yurt, Adam was snoring loudly. I sat up in my sleeping bag and tried to calm down, but as I shivered in the cold I wished I were back in my cottage in the Cotswolds, with a normal job and a regular income. I no longer understood why I had sold my house and given up my job and moved to Scotland to spend all my money on this madcap scheme. I was sure I had completely fucked up my whole life. When the experiment was over I would be destitute and homeless.

Everything seemed different compared to when I had first arrived, in July. When I looked around me in the

Barn, it no longer felt like a cosy place to bake bread and eat supper. It was a fucking mess. Dark, musty and shabby, piled high with the remnants of my former life – a plate here, a cup there – it was a grotesque reminder of my craziness. This cup once sat on a beautiful pine shelf in my kitchen. This plate was once part of a set that I used when I had friends over to dinner in the long Cotswold summer evenings. None of the volunteers saw it this way, of course. These objects held no emotional connotations for them. And the gap between their perception and mine made me feel incredibly alone.

The whole experiment now struck me as a farce. It was taking much longer to become self-sufficient than I had anticipated, so we were still making regular runs to the supermarket to buy food to supplement our meagre crop. At first I had justified these shopping trips in terms of our scenario by arguing that in the immediate aftermath of a global catastrophe, the survivors would be able to scavenge supplies from local houses and abandoned shops. But the grace period offered by the leftovers of civilization would only last so long, and the survivors would have to make sure they could grow or catch all their own food by the time the packaged stuff ran out. Now, almost a year into the experiment, every trip to the supermarket felt like a betrayal. How valuable a simulation of life after the collapse of civilization could it be, if we were still popping down to Tesco every week?

To address this problem, and recover some sort of equilibrium, I came up with the concept of Post-

Apocalyptic rating, or PA rating for short. If some activity or thing had a PA rating of 100 per cent it meant that it could be done, or could exist, in exactly the same way after the crash. Baked potatoes, for example, would have a PA rating of 100 per cent because we could grow our own potatoes, and bake them, without the need for any complex equipment that would eventually break and be impossible to repair. But a recipe that contained ingredients that could not be grown locally would have a lower PA rating. Lemon juice and olive oil, for example, would be unavailable in Scotland once modern transport links had broken down.

When we went shopping we would try not to buy anything with a PA rating of less than 100 per cent, so that even if we didn't in fact grow it or make it ourselves, we could at least have done so in theory. But even when we stuck to this plan, the very fact that we were going shopping felt to me like cheating. The whole experiment began to seem like a sham, an extended camping trip, a bunch of soft-skinned Westerners kidding themselves that they were hardy backwoodsmen while all around them lay the trappings of urban life.

Apparently, the Unabomber fared no better. Kevin Kelly, the founding editor of *Wired* magazine, remarks that the Unabomber's story collapses into the same ironic conclusion: even in his lonely Montana log cabin, he too lived off the fat of civilization:

The Unabomber's shack was crammed with stuff he purchased from the machine: snowshoes, boots, sweat shirts, food, explosives, mattresses, plastic jugs and buckets, etc. – all things that he could have made himself, but did not. After 25 years on the job, why did he not make his own tools separate from the system? It looks like he shopped at Wal-Mart. The food he scavenged from the wild was minimal. Instead he regularly rode his bike to town and there rented an old car to drive to the big city to restock his food and supplies from supermarkets. He was either incapable of supporting himself without civilization, or unwilling to.

The trips to the supermarket didn't seem to worry the volunteers, however, or dent their faith in the realism of the simulation. They went about their daily tasks with undimmed enthusiasm, as I watched in silent horror, unable or unwilling to tell them that the emperor was naked.

As I lost faith in the experiment, everyone else seemed to become even more committed. Agric was more convinced than ever that the first signs of global collapse were imminent. Pete and Tommy began to question the time-limited nature of the experiment. Why shut it all down after eighteen months, when we had put so much work into cultivating the land and building the yurts? Why not stay here indefinitely? It wouldn't be long until civilization really did collapse anyway. And when it did, this would be a pretty good place to be, if we wanted to survive.

Just when I had ensnared them all in my delusion, I found I no longer believed in it myself. And it had slipped away as mysteriously as it had first taken root. But this liberation was not pleasant. On the contrary, it left me feeling deflated and broken.

'We do not adopt a belief because it is true,' wrote E. M. Cioran, 'but because some obscure power impels us to do so. When this power leaves us, we suffer prostration and collapse, a tête-à-tête with what is left of ourselves.' Some obscure power had impelled me to believe in the imminent collapse of civilization, and that power had now left me as mysteriously as it had arrived. And the result was just as Cioran described; I suffered prostration and collapse. Mad though it may have been, that belief had kept me going for a year and a half. It had given me a reason to live, an energy that at times bordered on the manic, and a feeling of invincibility. It had carried me up to Scotland and protected me throughout the cold winter months. And now, in springtime, it had deserted me. I could still accept that civilization might collapse some time in the next hundred years or so, but it certainly wasn't going to come crashing down in the next year or two. Hell, it might even last another millennium.

I now think of that realization as the start of my recovery, but at the time it seemed like the beginning of my madness. From then on I began to sink deeper and deeper into the darkest depression of my life, and to those around me I looked increasingly pathetic and incompetent, like someone who had suddenly lost his way in life. But the way I had lost was a road to oblivion, and though I was now off-road, and wandering around in the wilderness, at least I wasn't heading directly towards the apocalypse any longer. The route out of the wilderness would take me through a dark valley, and even into a psychiatric hospital, but that was part of the recovery, and it would eventually lead me out of the woods and back into the bright daylight of sanity. The real madness was already over.

Now that Adam had gone, Agric began to assume a more dominant role, coordinating our efforts to grow vegetables, ensuring the header tank that fed the back boiler on the Rayburn was always topped up, and directing preparations for the evening meal. He was constantly on his feet, scampering around with a nervous energy that was by turns amusing and exasperating – exasperating because sometimes it seemed like activity for activity's sake.

'Agric never stops!' Johanna whispered to me. A sixty-seven-year-old retired biology teacher living in Edinburgh, she had a Nordic accent that complemented her aura of dignified solemnity. But now and again she would beam a huge smile that immediately dissolved any sense of distance. Johanna was at the experiment for only a few weeks. The revolving-door policy of the experiment was another reason why I now began to doubt its validity.

On the one hand, allowing people to come for a short period permitted a much greater variety of volunteers to join in. If I had insisted that everyone had to stay for several months, let alone the whole experiment, it would probably have been full of dropouts in their twenties (and the occasional older dropout, like Adam). We certainly wouldn't have had retired grandmothers like Johanna, with family obligations, or young people with big plans like Nick Stenning, or former marines like David Ross. And the diversity was important because the scenario we were acting out envisioned a group of strangers coming together to ride out the collapse of civilization together.

On the other hand, the shorter their stay, the less invested people were in the project. It's hard to get excited about digging and planting if you're not going to see the crops grow or eat them. Also, when people stayed for just a couple of weeks, they didn't get quite dirty enough to summon up the courage to use our primitive bathing facilities. So we lost out on the sense of gradual decline that would surely set in if people were here for longer – people arrived with fresh clothes and all their teeth, and left with only slightly dirty clothes and all their teeth.

Only the hardened utopians who stayed for longer than a few weeks could get fully into the spirit of this primitive way of life. By the time he had been on site for six weeks, Agric was no longer fazed by the whisky barrel bathtub and its rank odour. And after three months, the bottom half of one of Adam's front teeth broke off. I drove him to the nearest dentist but he couldn't get free care because he wasn't registered on any database. I paid for a quick fix, but the cheap dental crown came off again a few days later, so he just threw it away. At first this made him look a bit scary when he grinned, but we soon got used to it, and then it just gave him more character.

By now, we were making our own toothpaste by mixing baking powder, sea salt and peppermint, and rubbing it onto our teeth with our fingers. But we had no idea how to make the baking powder ourselves, so were still buying that at the supermarket. To be really authentic, we would have had to resort to more primitive measures, such as chewing sticks and twigs, as many people still do in India, but none of us went that far. Benjamin Franklin's toothpaste was a mixture of honey and ground charcoal, but that probably didn't keep the cavities away.

We also tried making our own soap, with variable success. First we would take some of the lard we had carefully stored after killing one of the pigs, and render it by boiling it up with water and letting the fat rise to the top as the mixture cooled overnight. The solid layer of grease floating on top the next morning was much cleaner than lard, since the impurities were left in the water below.

Next, we would take a large wooden bucket whose bottom had fallen out and place it on a stone slab down by the stream. We put a layer of grass and small sticks at the base of the bucket, and then covered it with wood ash from the Rayburn. Finally, we would gently pour water over the ashes and collect the brownish liquid (lye) that oozed out of the bottom of the bucket over the stone slab.

The last step was to mix the lye with the fat and boil the mixture over an open fire until it thickened into a frothy brew. As it boiled, we would throw some salt in to ensure that the cake of soap that formed on top would be hard, otherwise we would end up with a soft brown jelly which, while it functioned well enough as a cleaning material, was too far removed from the soap we remembered from civilization for most people's taste. It was a lot of effort, but at least we could pride ourselves on mastering this particular element of post-apocalyptic living.

It's the little things like toilet paper and toothpaste and soap, things that you hardly notice when you go about your daily life in rich countries, that you don't think about when you merely *imagine* what life might be like after the collapse of civilization. It's only when you start acting it out – when you start trying to live as if civilization has already collapsed – that these little details intrude. And these details turn out to matter much more than you might think.

I was beginning to lose track of who was supposed to be coming and when. I had drawn up a schedule while I was still in England, coordinating everything by email with the volunteers, but in the meantime some people had pulled out, while others wanted to come at different times, and my paper notes were now a mess. Agric kindly offered to take over the task, and we set up an old computer in the Barn for him to communicate with the forthcoming arrivals.

the computer was another compromise with the modern world. I tried to justify its presence on the grounds that we might be able to keep some electronic devices going for the first few years after civilization collapsed. But what about the Internet? Nick Stenning, the gap year student who had cut his finger, had suggested the net might survive in some form for a while. The infrastructure on which the Internet is built is pretty centralized and therefore quite fragile, but wireless networking might offer a decentralized, more organic alternative, similar to the way mobile phone networks operate. There is still a certain level of hierarchy with cell phones, in the sense that each cell is operated by a mast. In theory, however, a call can bounce from cell to cell without being rerouted through a central hub. Ad-hoc wireless networks can be formed of computers too. A group of wireless computers can talk to each other (often through other members of the group) without any real hub. And it was this kind of network, Nick argued, that anyone preparing for the collapse of civilization should try and enhance. There are no cables to maintain, no natural disasters to guard against (in the sense that you only have to protect the computers, not the infrastructure connecting them – that's just air).

I was intrigued by Nick's thoughts on post-apocalyptic networking. What would it be like to live in a world in which people had largely returned to low-tech pre-industrial technology but still had a few computers hooked up to the Internet? The pre-industrial world seemed, in many respects, so much more appealing than the industrial one, but it clearly had several major defects, one of which was its parochialism and the great difficulty of spreading good ideas. A pre-industrial world with Internet access might have the best of both worlds.

But this rosy image of laptops in tree-houses was, of course, beset by the same problems that cast a shadow over Tommy's suggestion that we could simply wander around gathering used iPods. Sooner or later the computers would break down, and without a modern technological infrastructure we wouldn't be able to repair them. So even if we kept some kind of limited network going for a while, it wouldn't last very long.

Perhaps we could take advantage of this grace period to copy down the most important bits of knowledge from the web before it disappeared completely. Assuming we had a supply of paper and pens, we could work like medieval scribes, preserving the hard won knowledge of our ancestors for posterity. But what, exactly, would we choose to preserve? Would it be best to focus on purely practical things, like which plants were poisonous, and how to make soap? Or would it be worth including some more abstract stuff too, like the periodic table and the germ theory of disease? Millions of our ancestors died because they didn't realize that some diseases can be transmitted by organisms that are too small for the naked eye to see, so it would be useful to keep at least some scientific discoveries as well as the more practical bits of knowhow.

But when Angus wanted to use the computer to check Facebook, I baulked. The computer was only for organizing the volunteers, I insisted. It wasn't really supposed to be part of the experiment itself.

'That's a moot point,' said Angus, shaking his head. 'I'm not really clear about what is and what isn't part of the experiment any more, Dylan. Are you?'

For one week in mid-May the weather was unusually benign – sunny days that made the Highlands look like Switzerland in June. But the week after there was torrential rain, and the weather turned bitterly cold. Our latest arrival – a former medical physicist who had opted out of the rat race a few years before, and now divided her time between a flat in Edinburgh and a caravan in southern France – was, quite rightly, miserable.

'I've lived in Scotland for twenty-four years,' said Georgia, 'and I know what cold is. This is cold! Lying in a sleeping bag under two duvets and a blanket and still having cold feet is cold in anyone's language.'

'But you're still here!' I said, impressed with her stoicism.

'I don't know any other woman who would be!' she said. 'But I'm not scared. I've got more bloody bottle than that.'

But the following day the yurt she was sleeping in began to leak. We tied a cord to the corners of a bit of plastic and slung it over the top of the yurt. It seemed to work, but it didn't look like it would last very long.

Agric was still smiling. 'Isn't it wonderful, though, this kind of lifestyle?' he chided. 'Doesn't it make you see how your normal life isn't as good as you thought?'

'Certainly not!' replied Georgia. 'My normal life is fabulous!'

Though volunteers came and went, the number of people living on site at any one time gradually increased, and by now there were usually between eight and twelve. As a result, we were using a lot more wood. The pot-bellied stoves in the three yurts were banked up with logs every evening, the Rayburn was going through fuel at an awful rate, and we also wanted to build more structures, such as a cold storage cellar under the ground (using wooden planks to line the earth walls). There was no way our little patch of woodland could cater for all our needs. The experiment had already become unsustainable, at least in terms of trees. Like the Maya, we had exceeded the carrying capacity of our local environment. But unlike the Maya, we had the Forestry Commission, so I called them and ordered seventeen tons of logs.

The wood was delivered early one frosty morning. I had lain awake all night, worrying what would happen when my money ran out, wondering whether I would be trapped in Utopia forever, when I heard the deep growl of a large engine grow louder and louder. I pulled on my trousers, and trudged up the side of the little valley to the higher ground where Gertrude stood. And there I was confronted by a horrifying sight.

The Forestry Commission had not delivered the little blocks I was expecting, but a dozen or so whole tree trunks. They were massive things, sixteen feet long and almost two feet in diameter, tall Scots pines felled by huge harvesting machines, and piled on the back of a fearsome articulated lorry. I watched, speechless, as the driver unloaded the trunks one by one with the boom crane attached to the truck, and piled them up in an imposing stack that dwarfed my puny little body. When he had finished, he hopped down and asked if I was happy.

All I could do was nod my head and stammer: 'I . . .

I . . . thought they would be smaller . . .' I wasn't even able to muster a smile.

It was only when the lorry had disappeared that it dawned on me that the tree trunks rested on a gentle slope, and were stacked in such a way that they might roll downhill if, somehow, they were dislodged. If they did start rolling, they would quickly pick up speed and smash Gertrude to pieces, and then cascade down the valley onto the small blue yurts below. From then on, I was terrified that the pile would collapse in the middle of the night. I had visions of being crushed to death by a stray Scots pine while I was sleeping.

Once again, my worries about something external collapsing distracted me from my own psychological collapse, that was by now a far more clear and present danger. The tree trunks symbolized my loss of control, my sense of powerlessness to prevent a looming disaster. Only this can explain my apparently exaggerated reaction to their sudden appearance. When Romay appeared, to find me frozen to the spot, my face white with horror, she couldn't suppress a little giggle.

Our newly abundant supply of wood encouraged us to develop our woodworking skills. A local couple called Paddy and Sue were old hands at green carpentry and came to teach us the basics. They were selling their house to take up a nomadic lifestyle, and asked if they could come and stay at Utopia at some point. They seemed to think of it as just another eco-village or hippy commune, rather than an experiment in post-apocalyptic living, but I was too despondent to try and change their minds.

Paddy and Sue were enthusiastic about working without power tools. They laid out their implements like surgeons preparing for an operation – a side-axe, a drawknife, adzes and mallets – and unveiled their shave horse, so-called because the user sits astride it. Then they led us into the woodland down by the river on a search for suitable raw materials, and we came back with some branches of ash and cherry.

We began by cutting the branches to length with a coarse saw, and then hewed the wood into rough billets with the axes and adzes, always working with the grain. With the longer billets, which we planned to use for chair legs, we would clamp them to the shave horse and shape them with a drawknife. With the shorter pieces, we would just whittle them into shape with a pocket knife. Graham, a twenty-one-year-old architecture student from Sheffield with floppy brown hair, who had just arrived in Utopia the previous day, was soon happily whittling a spoon. Everyone seemed to be having fun except me. This was exactly the sort of thing I had looked forward to when I started planning the experiment, and yet now I felt joyless and empty.

That evening a few friends of Paddy and Sue arrived in an old jeep and an impromptu party sprang into life. The weather was glorious and Graham gathered some wood for a bonfire. Then, Paddy's friends took a chainsaw out of their jeep and sawed a length of wood about three feet long off the end of one of the huge tree trunks that had been delivered by the Forestry Commission. Two people then wrestled the stump over to near the bonfire, and set it upright. They cut four deep grooves in the top, in the shape of a cross, and put some shavings in the centre of the grooves, and lit them. As the flames burned down into the grooves, the tree stump sent out flames, shooting up like fireworks, which gave out more heat than the bonfire. The volunteers cheered.

I tried to look happy but inside I was numb. 'What a terrible waste of wood,' I thought.

By the time Heather came to Utopia to teach us how to identify the medicinal plants that grew wild around the river, I was no longer myself. I felt as though the ground had been pulled from under my feet, and I was falling, falling, falling, with nothing to grab on to and no idea when, or if, I would ever land.

But nobody else seemed to notice, or if they did, they kept quiet about it. I felt like screaming, but no sound would come out. My eyes, I was sure, had the wild, desperate look of a man who has just been told he will be shot at dawn. And yet everyone went about their business as if nothing had happened, as if everything was normal. I felt invisible.

So when Heather arrived, and walked around Utopia with us, bending down now and again to point out a plant, or a flower, and describe its various uses and healing properties, all I could do was to follow mutely along and pretend I understood.

'This is wood sorrel. You can make tea from an infusion of the leaves to treat fever and colds.'

The volunteers were fascinated, and nibbled the leaf that Heather passed round to see what it tasted like. But none of this seemed real to me.

'This is goosegrass, or cleavers. It has a soothing effect which can help with insomnia.'

I struggled to make out the identifying features of the plant, but it looked like, well, it looked like just another plant.

'This is sweet cicely. It's good for treating coughs. But be careful not to confuse it with hemlock! The little white flowers look very similar, but hemlock is a deadly poison.'

And then it struck me. If only I could find some hemlock! That would be my way out of Utopia. If it was good enough for Socrates (the philosopher, not the cat), it was good enough for me.

From that moment on, thoughts of suicide began to recur with increasing frequency. I contemplated hanging myself in the woods, but that was too dramatic, and it would be better anyway if I could make it look like an accident. I thought about sleeping outside on a cold night to get hypothermia, but that wouldn't be quick enough, and the volunteers might try to save me. I kept coming back to hemlock, which definitely seemed the best solu-

tion – if only I could find some. It's harder to kill yourself
in the wild than in an urban setting, where bridges, cars
and trains provide plenty of opportunities.

But deep down, I think I always knew that I didn't
have the courage. It takes guts to put an end to your life,
and a decisiveness that I once had but was now completely lacking. I bumbled along, incapable of making the
smallest decision, let alone a momentous one like suicide.
And I could see no way out of Utopia, no place to land,
and nothing to put an end to my free fall.

Apart from Bo, the only other person I confided in about
my rapidly worsening state of mind was my friend Chris.
I had broken my rule about only using the Internet for
Utopia business and sent him an email. My ability to
concentrate had diminished to the point where I was
only able to write a few lines. But they must have been
enough to convey some idea of my sense of helplessness
and despair, for Chris immediately bought me a plane
ticket to London, so he could look after me for a week
at his house in Catford.

Miserable though I was in Utopia, I was loath to take
another break. I had already spent time with Scott and
Jules after my crisis at open day, and now I was at the
cottage every other night with Bo, so the idea of spending a whole week away on top of all that felt deeply
disloyal. The volunteers might come and go, but I was
supposed to be there throughout the experiment, fully

immersed in my alternative reality. But that was clearly no longer the case, and Chris tried to reassure me that this was the best thing I could do to make the project a success. Even the volunteers agreed I needed a break. But all the same, I felt guilty about going away.

A few days later, Angus drove me to the airport. I was fidgeting nervously in the passenger seat, so he tried to cheer me up by reminding me about some of the good times we had spent together.

'Do you remember that time when we went to the Notting Hill Carnival together, and you got waylaid by that really fat girl?' he said, smirking.

I nodded silently, and forced a smile.

'She would have eaten you for breakfast!' Angus chuckled.

'Thanks for coming up here and helping out,' I stammered.

'No worries, mate! You were a real support to me when I was in Germany, remember? Your phone calls were the only thing that kept me sane.'

'Yes, I remember,' I said weakly. I turned and looked at him. He had been through some tough times too, but he looked strong and happy now. I envied his sense of self-assurance, his devil-may-care attitude. I wondered if I would ever be like that again.

'Am I doing the right thing, going away?' I asked.

'Yeah, of course you are! Everybody needs a break now and again. And, to be honest, I think everyone needs a break from you.'

'Maybe I shouldn't go. Maybe you should turn round and drive me back,' I whimpered.

'No! I'm not turning round. You're getting on that flight!'

I was so reluctant to go he almost had to push me out of the car.

'Come on, off you go! It'll be good for you!' Angus said, trying to be patient, but looking rather weary.

I opened the car door with one hand, but gripped firmly on to the seat with the other.

'What's wrong with me?' I pleaded.

Angus smiled. 'It's simple. You wanted to get outside your comfort zone, and now you are, and you don't bloody like it!'

I got out of the car and walked to the terminal building. It felt alien and futuristic, as if I had arrived from the distant past in a time machine. I fidgeted throughout the whole flight.

When Chris greeted me at arrivals in Heathrow, his jaw dropped. I was, he said, thin and pale, and looked as if I had walked all the way from Scotland. Back at his house, he had made up a little bed for me in his spare room. He had prepared some supper, but all I wanted to do was sleep.

Each day that week, as I crawled out of my bed and made my way downstairs for breakfast, I would look up admiringly at the rows of coloured paper pinned to the walls of the stairway. Chris wrote textbooks for a living, and each piece of paper had a list of milestones that he had set himself for each book. Every milestone had been dutifully ticked off as he had achieved them. These humble records spoke eloquently of his patient setting of goals, and his diligent accomplishment of each one. And they felt like a silent rebuke of my way of living.

Chris and I both wrote books, but we worked in very different ways. I would write furiously for a few months, finish a book, and then not write again until I had blown my advance on holidays, DJ equipment, or some ill-conceived project. And then I would return to my desk to write another book. My Utopia Experiment was just the latest and biggest blowout.

Chris, on the other hand, had been writing for several hours every day for the past ten years. In that time, he had steadily built up a small fortune. He was always talking about retiring to the country, but he never seemed to think he had enough money to take the plunge. Even now, with perhaps a million pounds in the bank and large royalty cheques arriving every few months, he was still living in his run-down old house in Catford. I used to chide him about this, wondering out loud if he would ever actually make the move. But now his inertia no longer seemed so risible, and I even fancied I caught the occasional gleam of triumph in Chris's eyes, as if my downtrodden air was the vindication he had always been seeking that his way of life was better than mine.

I proceeded to indulge in an orgy of remorse for my

former ways. Whenever Chris asked how I was doing, all I could do was to whisper, over and over again: 'Why did I sell my house? Why did I give up my job? Why did I sell my house?' Chris had the patience of a saint, but after a few days even he was getting worn down by my repetitious monologue. 'That's all in the past now, Dylan,' he would say; 'you've got to put it behind you and move on.' I knew that, of course, but all the same I couldn't help repeating my mantra ad nauseam: 'Why did I sell my house? Why did I give up my job?'

'Come on, Dylan, snap out of it! This isn't doing you any good!'

'But I've fucked up my whole life,' I whined.

'No you haven't. The experiment isn't going too badly. Think of everything you've achieved there already.'

But when I recalled the dirty, dingy, musty old Barn, and the cold, damp nights in the yurts, I didn't feel any pride.

'And I'm sure you'll come out of this a much stronger and wiser person,' he said. 'Maybe you will discover your true self, like in that birthday card I gave you. Remember?'

I did remember. The card showed a young man hiking in the mountains. He is dressed like a typical backpacker, and wears a hippyish beard. He looks surprised, for on the path ahead, and looking straight back at him, is a man dressed in a smart suit and holding a briefcase. And this man has the same face as the hippy, minus the beard.

Below the cartoon, Chris had Tippexed out one of the

words in the caption, and written my name there instead, so that it read: 'Halfway up the Himalayas, Dylan finally discovered his true self.'

And in a way, that summed up one of the most galling lessons that the Utopia Experiment taught me. No matter how hard I tried, I wasn't the rugged survivalist I had imagined myself to be. I just didn't have it in me. There, halfway up Mount Utopia, I had indeed discovered my true self. And he wasn't Grizzly Adams. He was wearing a suit.

It wasn't that I wore suits very often before I started the Utopia Experiment. In fact I hardly wore suits at all. But I was just as incapable of surviving in the wild as any city dweller. I may have fancied I could turn my hand to anything. But the truth is it takes lots of time and practice to learn your way around a woodland, and know which plants to eat and which to avoid, and which trees provide the best wood for different uses, and how to track an animal, and how to build shelter and start a fire. I had arrogantly assumed I could pick up all these skills as quickly as I could master a new academic discipline or understand a scientific theory. But I couldn't; book learning and hands-on survival skills require very different kinds of mental faculties.

But there was one sense in which the birthday card wasn't right at all. I was never an organization man. The same visual trope was featured in an ad that DuPont ran not long after William H. Whyte's seminal work *The Organization Man* was published in 1956. In the upper right-hand corner of the ad a handful of men dressed in look-alike suits stride purposefully towards some unseen office. In the bottom left-hand corner sits a solitary figure, 'Bernie the Beatnik', in sandals and jeans, holding a guitar. Across the top of the ad ran the headline, 'The Organization, Man!'

Some smaller text below voiced Bernie the Beatnik's refusal to take a job in a big company: 'Go to work every day, do what you're told, lose your freedom!' he exclaims. That's pretty much how I felt about working in academia, and it's why I quit. I had found that universities were no different from any other large organization; the same timid conformity, the same stifling bureaucracy, was equally present in those supposed temples of creative thought and free expression as in the most faceless corporation. And in that sense, I really was the hippy in the birthday card, not the suited gentleman. Outwardly I may have looked like an organization man, but inside I had always been Bernie the Beatnik.

And, curiously, that fed into my disenchantment with Utopia. For all its outward eccentricity, the little community had by now become as conformist as any corporation. Nobody questioned the idea that civilization was about to collapse. Everyone agreed that the modern world was an increasingly grim place, and looked forward to the coming crash. Groupthink had spread through Utopia like a virus, infecting everyone except Adam. He alone had remained resolutely difficult, a stubborn and obstinate bastard. And that was why I liked him, and felt so distant from the others.

Romay was there to pick me up at the airport when I flew back from London. Angus, she said, had gone back down to England.

I was no better, psychologically, than when I had left the week before. I was just as jittery, and I still wore the same wide-eyed expression, looking permanently like someone whose face has just been slapped with a wet fish. I told Romay I couldn't face going straight back to Utopia, and asked her to drop me at Bo's cottage.

When Bo opened the door she stood there for a few moments without saying a word. And then we had a conversation that ended our relationship.

13. COLLAPSE

Breaking up with Bo was an emotional blow, but I consoled myself with the thought that I could now spend all my time at Utopia, instead of dashing back to Bo's cottage every few days. Rather than lifting a weight from my shoulders, however, my less sporadic presence at Utopia only made my mood darken further. I now felt trapped, and when any of the volunteers tried to engage me in conversation, I never knew what to reply. I would stand there in silence for a few moments, then make some hasty excuse and shuffle off. I might occasionally try to join in the daily work, chopping firewood or weeding the vegetable patch, only to find myself paralysed. Ashamed of myself, I took to wandering off into the woods to hide, hoping that nobody would come and find me brooding under a tree, or curled up by the little waterfall. I was even less present than I had been before.

In the first week of June, a group of three film students from London arrived to make a short documentary about the experiment for their final year project. Camilla, Tony and Ryan looked very incongruous as they paced around Utopia with their high-tech camera equipment. They had visited several months before, when I was still well, and they were shocked to find a very different Dylan, no longer confident and energetic, but now downtrodden, dejected and listless.

This only made for a more interesting film. A documentary about an experiment in post-apocalyptic living was already a good start, but to show the founder coming unstuck and undergoing some sort of psychological meltdown added an extra twist. It was a pretty classic story, of course. A mad scientist who creates a bizarre experiment and then goes off the rails? Hardly original, but then it's always the old plots that work best.

As they walked around, filming bits here and there, I felt like the Savage from *Brave New World*, whose quest for isolation is thwarted by dozens of gawking sightseers, intrigued by his weird behaviour. When they filmed me chopping wood, I could barely even hit the log, let alone split it cleanly down the middle. I was uncoordinated, feeble and pathetic. When they interviewed me, I tried to give the impression that everything was going just fine, but my voice was hoarse and low, with no breath left in it.

Tony was from South Africa. He had worked for Reuters and reported from Somalia and Zimbabwe. He looked upon the Utopia Experiment with the eyes of someone who had seen real disasters and real poverty.

'If you want to see what life is like after peak oil,' he said, 'all you have to do is look at Africa.'

He was right; they already lived with scarcity, while we play-acted unconvincingly, our kitchen shelves stocked with five different kinds of vegetable oil and packs of rare spices, which previous volunteers had brought with them and left behind. Agric's pot of Gardener's Relief hand cream sitting on the table said it all.

Nor was it the first time I had been confronted with such criticisms. When I had first arrived in Scotland a friend had pointed out the parallels with Marx's critique of utopian socialism. Wasn't I just as naive as Charles Fourier or Robert Owen, a self-satisfied bourgeois playing at paradise while the rest of the world went to hell in a handcart? Real societies out there in the world were actually dealing with reconstruction after social breakdown, so wasn't it in fact rather distasteful to play at it?

Back then, I had tried to justify my experiment by arguing that it wasn't simply any kind of social breakdown that I was interested in, but a particular one – namely, the collapse of our globalized late-industrial civilization, with all the attendant breakdown of government, finance and trade. And while it was true that there were societies out there in the world actually dealing with reconstruction, the breakdown suffered by those societies was limited in geographical scope and thus very different to the global collapse I envisaged. As long as social breakdown was confined to one country or region, other countries could provide assistance; some forms of stable currency would remain to those who could afford them; international transport links would remain in place. But if breakdown propagated through the whole global system, aftermath would be very different.

Was it distasteful for affluent Westerners to play at imagining such things? I didn't think so at first, but now I wasn't so sure. When it was *just* play, it was perhaps OK. There's nothing wrong with play, and I had hoped it would be lots of fun. But it wasn't really fun any more, and the volunteers increasingly thought of it less as play and more as a dress rehearsal. In their minds it was morphing from a simulation of what life *might* be like if civilization collapsed, into a real-life preparation for an imminent catastrophe, just as it had in mine beforehand.

While Camilla, Tony and Ryan were still at Utopia, finishing off their film project, my friend Lewis came to visit. I had known him since we were students at Southampton University together, and he was now a professor of archaeology.

Lewis was in rude health. He had been working out, and his shoulders were broader. I, on the other hand, was painfully thin, and my clothes hung limply about me, like a baggy jumper on a scarecrow. Lewis looked shocked when he first saw me.

'My god, Dylan, you look terrible!' he gasped.

I managed a weak grin. 'It's not easy surviving the apocalypse,' I said.

I showed Lewis around Utopia, and he seemed vaguely impressed, but I wasn't sure whether he was just being polite. He had thought of staying in the yurts like everyone else, but when he poked his nose into one and saw the jumbled mass of sleeping bags and smelt the musty odour, he decided he would sleep at Romay's farmhouse instead.

The next day, Lewis decided he would rent a car and drive up to the Orkney Islands to visit Skara Brae, a stone-built Neolithic settlement located on the west coast of Mainland, the largest island in the Orkney archipelago. Camilla, Tony and Ryan were going with him, and they all wanted me to come along too, but once again I felt hesitant about leaving Utopia. I hated every minute I spent there, but the idea of leaving didn't seem to promise any relief. On the contrary, it terrified me.

Eventually Lewis cajoled me into getting in the car with him and the others, and we drove to Scrabster, on the northernmost edge of Scotland, where we would take the ferry to Stromness. But as we drove, I could feel myself becoming increasingly anxious, and I begged Lewis to turn round and drop me back at Utopia.

'Don't be silly, Dylan. Relax! This is going to be fun,' said Lewis.

'Please, Lewis, please!' I pleaded. 'Please take me back! I need to get back!'

'Really?'

'Yes, really! Please please please take me back.'

Lewis pulled over to the side of the road and did a U-turn. And then, after we had been heading back down south for a few minutes, I let out a deep sigh.

'It's OK, Lewis, I'm fine now. I want to see Skara Brae with you. Please turn round, will you?'

Lewis looked at me with growing impatience. 'OK,' he said, 'but I'm not turning round any more. If you ask me to take you back to Utopia again, I'm going to ignore you.'

I nodded meekly, and Lewis turned the car back round again. When we finally got to Scrabster, we had just missed the ferry by about five minutes.

'Damn!' said Lewis. 'I wanted to spend the night in Stromness so we could get up early to visit Skara Brae. We'll have to stay here now, and get the first ferry tomorrow morning.'

I don't know what the film students made of my strange behaviour. They were very gracious about missing the ferry, and didn't say a word of blame. We found a cheap guesthouse, and then went out for some fish and chips. I hadn't eaten chips for months, and I savoured every one, dipping them in mayonnaise and ketchup like a little kid. Lewis looked at me and shook his head slowly.

'It's not really a scientific experiment at all, is it, this Utopia thing?' he said. 'I mean, a real scientific experiment has to have hypotheses. What are your hypotheses?'

I winced, and pulled a crumpled piece of paper out of my pocket. Scrawled on it were a few lines of spidery handwriting, in which I had tried to sum up the main axioms on which the experiment was predicated. I had written it while I was staying with Chris, in a vain attempt to remember what I was doing, and why, and I had kept it with me ever since, like a talisman. I gave it to Lewis. It read:

> Global civilization is going to collapse within our lifetimes due to global warming and the energy crisis (peak oil).
>
> When civilization collapses, billions of people will die, but some people will survive.
>
> It will be impossible to rebuild civilization. Those who survive will have to escape to the wild, form tribes, and learn survival skills. This process is called 'rewilding' or 'de-industrialization' or 'the New Tribal Revolution'.
>
> Rewilding will improve our quality of life compared to how it was before the crash.

Lewis read it over several times and gazed into the distance, pondering what I had written.

'So that's your main hypothesis,' he said, at last. 'Getting back to nature would make you happy.'

'I guess so,' I whispered.

'Well that didn't work out so well, did it?'

When we got back to Utopia a few days later, another volunteer had arrived. James Durston, a tall young man with short brown hair, was brimming with self-confidence. He was in his late twenties, and had recently moved to India, but was back in the UK for a few weeks, and curious to see what we were up to in Scotland. He had brought some authentic Indian spices with him, which now sat incongruously next to our porridge oats on a shelf in the Barn.

James plunged into the experiment with gusto. Within a day he had discovered that dandelion roots and stinging nettles made nutritious side dishes when cooked correctly. A few days later and he was baking his own bread and making dinner for nine people. Two weeks in and he had built a bunk-bed, made a chess set and put up a sturdy support for a clutch of runner beans. He loved being outside, even when it was cold and rainy, and he would dig and weed and water the vegetable patch for hours each day.

James was keen to spread the word about Utopia, and persuaded the *Independent*, a national newspaper, to let him write a feature about the experiment for them. It was published while I was in hospital, and when I read it, I was devastated. His warm recollections of communal life barely registered; in the self-absorbed way that is typical of depression, all I could see were his remarks about me, towards the end of the article. 'Evans,' he wrote, 'has come and gone, physically and mentally, since the project began.' It was true, of course, but I didn't want the whole world to know about my impaired mental state, and my heart sank when I thought what my former colleagues and students, or my friends and family, would think if they read it. I could see the smug expressions of 'I told you so' on their faces, as they shook their heads, and pitied me for throwing away my career and my money on such a foolish venture. 'In fact,' James added, 'Dylan is the one thing that could dismantle the entire experiment.' I resented James for putting that in. Why couldn't he have spared me the shame and just focused on the volunteers?

As it was, the volunteers seemed happy enough. 'It is unlikely,' wrote James, 'that Dylan's mental hibernation will dramatically disrupt the day-to-day workings of the project, though it is frustrating for those on the ground.' I hadn't actually noticed their frustration, though I did wonder. I was too afraid to ask them, too afraid I had let them down, but they must have been disappointed when, instead of engaging with the routine activities, I simply hung around in a daze, occasionally picking up an axe or a shovel, only to put it down a few minutes later after achieving nothing. They had every right to expect some kind of leadership on my part, but by June I was barely capable of making conversation, let alone giving direction.

'Ultimately,' James concluded, 'I suppose it will be Dylan Evans himself who learns the most from this project.'

I think he was right about that too.

One cloudy afternoon in late June, a battered blue van spluttered into Utopia. The sweet smell of the exhaust fumes signalled that it was running on a mix of diesel and vegetable oil. I watched as two men got out, one in his thirties and the other in his twenties. Something about them – or was it me? – made me reluctant to give them a warm welcome.

'What do you want?' I muttered in a sullen tone of voice.

'We heard about what you're doing here,' said the older man. 'We thought we'd pay you a visit.'

I didn't feel like entertaining visitors. I could barely hold a normal conversation with the volunteers any more, let alone with a complete stranger. For a moment I was tempted to tell them to leave, but something inside me relented, and I invited them into the Barn.

Their names were Nick and Chris, they told us, when we were all sitting round the big table in the semi-darkness, sipping mugs of hot dandelion tea that Agric had laboriously prepared. Nick, the elder of the two, lived in the blue van, and grew vegetables on a fifteen-acre site devoted to community-supported agriculture. Chris lived in a caravan ('one step up from Nick,' he smiled) and worked on the same site. Between them they grew enough vegetables to feed two hundred people, which made our efforts look pathetic by comparison. Members of their box scheme paid at the onset of the growing season for a share of the anticipated harvest; once harvesting began, Nick and Chris would deliver a box to each subscriber with their weekly shares of vegetables and fruit.

This was so much more efficient than our attempts to grow our own food that I felt rather embarrassed when Nick and Chris asked about our crops. Their questions were probing and soon they had exposed many of the flaws in the experiment. Eighteen months was too short; why start a big project like this and then abandon it after just a couple of growing seasons? If people could come along for just a month, how would they be motivated to work hard for a harvest they wouldn't reap? How were we going to make our own clothes when the stuff we had salvaged from civilization had all begun to fall apart? Were we still shopping at Tesco?

I felt their questions sting like sea salt in a hundred scratches. They were right; my project wasn't nearly as rustic and authentic as I had anticipated. We still weren't self-sufficient, and even Agric's expertise in growing vegetables was no match for the knowledge of these two young men. They were doing it for real, and they had been for years, while we were just play-acting. I could sense their disdain, even though they tried to hide it, as we showed them our tiny vegetable patch, and when they asked me what was growing there, I couldn't even remember what half the crops were called. I really didn't have a clue what I was doing.

Meanwhile, the experiment rumbled along, carried forward by its own momentum. I felt paralysed, like someone watching from a distance while a train barrelled down a track towards a broken bridge, powerless to prevent the impending disaster. Everyone else seemed to get more enthusiastic as time went on, making it even harder for me to question out loud the value of what we were doing. I gazed on with silent horror while they went about their daily duties without a care in the world.

More volunteers arrived. Tobe and Ruth brought their two-year-old son. They too were convinced that civilization was going to collapse soon.

'We're selling our flat in London so we can become nomads,' they told me.

'Don't do it!' I felt like saying. 'It's a mistake! Civilization isn't going to collapse any time soon. I sold my house and I wish I hadn't!'

But that would have been like Jesus saying he didn't believe in God, or Moses saying the Promised Land was just a myth.

'We really like what you are doing here,' they said. 'We came here so we could learn a bit more about the food-growing side of things. We don't have much experience of that, and we figure we'll need to know about it when civilization collapses.'

Tobe was a sound engineer and had played in a couple of bands. Ruth was a sculptor. They had no survival skills, but they assumed they could pick it all up in a couple of weeks. They were as naive and unrealistic as I had been when I first thought up my experiment. I felt sorry for them, and I felt dishonest when I feigned a smile and nodded in mute assent.

Why did I no longer believe that civilization was in danger of imminent collapse? What led me to lose my faith in the apocalypse? I would like to say it was due to positive signs of change that began to appear on the horizon. But when I had heard some story beforehand, about some major corporation making efforts to reduce its carbon footprint, I had simply dismissed it as greenwash. So why did I now take such stories seriously?

I think my change of heart was due to a curious social dynamic. It has often been noted that beliefs tend to spread like viruses; as more and more people come to believe in something, those around them are more likely to adopt the belief. Psychologists call it the bandwagon effect. But with me, the opposite seemed to happen. The more those around me came to believe in the experiment, the more sceptical I became. Call it the difficult bastard effect.

This had happened on several previous occasions in my life. When I was nineteen I spent a year training to be a priest, only to discover that, unlike my fellow seminarians, I didn't really believe in God. Ten years later I thought I had discovered the ultimate truth in the writings of Jacques Lacan, only to recoil in horror when I had surrounded myself with his most ardent disciples. I was like a foolish bird that kept alighting on sticky twigs, all coated in birdlime to trap him. Through a combination of luck and sheer bloody-mindedness, I had always managed to struggle free and flutter away, only to spy another branch beckoning me from below. I never seemed to learn that each branch was as sticky as the last. Try as I might, I just could not find the perfect disappointment, the one that would finally kill that pernicious temptress, hope.

Now the same dynamic was undermining my beliefs about global collapse. As the volunteers became more convinced that disaster was imminent, I could see my own journey from speculation to conviction reflected in them like a mirror. As I came to see how stubborn and ridiculous their faith was, I realized how idiotic mine was too. When Agric dismissed the growing global awareness of climate change as mere window-dressing, I could see myself sneering at other objections that my friends had raised when I first told them about my own concerns. Like a religious fundamentalist immune to any evidence that might call his beliefs into question, I had clung to my faith in imminent catastrophe. The idea that our civilization might not only survive global warming but also continue to grow richer had appalled me, and this was perhaps why I had believed so ardently that it would collapse. I had *wanted* it to. Agric still did.

Never believe the evidence unless it is supported by a good theory. Or so said some wag, in a clever inversion of the standard view of how science works. And there is a lot of sense in approaching the world that way. We don't dismiss the whole of chemistry when a high school student gets an unexpected result in the lab. We simply assume that the student has made a mistake. If the theory is solid, it makes sense to reject the anomalous data rather than questioning the theory itself.

Part of the reason why Agric was so dismissive of any suggestion that civilization might not be about to collapse was the fact that he had a powerful theory. He was in the grip of Malthus, like many before him. Malthus had shown that population growth must always outstrip food supply, right? He had *proved* it.

A lot of the appeal of Malthusian reasoning lies in the apparent inescapability of the maths. That's what seems to have driven the fanatical conviction of the biologist Paul Ehrlich, who began his 1968 bestseller, *The Population Bomb*, with the dramatic claim that 'The battle to feed all of humanity is over. In the 1970s hundreds of millions of people will starve to death in spite of any crash programs embarked upon now. At this late date nothing can prevent a substantial increase in the world death rate.' The same apparently inexorable mathematical reasoning underpinned *The Limits to Growth*, a 1972 bestseller that made similar gloomy forecasts on the basis of fancy computer models.

If you accept the premises of Malthus's argument, the conclusions do of course follow with the iron necessity of logic. The problem is that fascination with the maths tends to drown out any consideration of whether the premises are, in fact, true or false. And there's the catch; for there's no compelling reason to believe that population growth must always outstrip food supply.

There is no such thing as a 'natural carrying capacity', because the environment that humans live in is not strictly natural. Since the birth of agriculture, humans have used technology to sustain populations well beyond levels that would be possible without it. Who knows what will be possible with the technologies of the future?

But Malthusians reject technological solutions as mere temporary fixes, and thereby reveal a deep mistrust of human ingenuity. Far from being the solution, 'our cleverness, our inventiveness,' says Stephen Emmott in his alarmist pamphlet *10 Billion*, 'are now the drivers of every global problem we face'.

Don't look to human intelligence, in other words, to *solve* our problems; it's precisely our curiosity that got us into trouble in the first place. Eve should never have eaten from the tree of knowledge. Prometheus should never have stolen fire from the gods. We should give up our arrogant belief in progress, and learn to say enough is enough.

And so the maths is just a fig leaf, a convenient distraction from the misanthropic spirit that really animates the merchants of doom. But it is a powerful soporific, and it hypnotizes many.

One morning I awoke to find myself curled up under some bushes, my clothes wet with the early morning dew. I can't say why I had fallen asleep there, but it was something to do with my madness. I crawled out from the ditch and stood up slowly, my body still stiff and sore from sleeping on the cold earth. It was a grey, misty morning, and it didn't look like there were any signs of life in Utopia, a few hundred metres further down the gently sloping hill. I trudged away in the opposite direction, towards Romay's farmhouse.

'What on earth have you been up to?' exclaimed Romay, when I stumbled into her kitchen, bedraggled and unkempt.

I said nothing, and slumped into a chair at the rustic kitchen table.

Romay shook her head, though whether in pity or disapproval I couldn't tell.

'I'll make you a cup of tea,' she said. 'Oh, and a letter came for you.'

Unenthusiastically, I opened the envelope and scanned the contents. It informed me that I had an appointment with a psychiatrist.

I had finally acknowledged my need for medical treatment a few weeks before, and been to see a local GP. But when I explained my predicament, he seemed out of his depth, and told me I needed to see a psychiatrist.

Romay seemed unimpressed. 'When is it?' she asked.

I looked up at her, blinking incredulously.

'Today,' I said.

An hour or so later, Romay drove me to the hospital.

'Do you want me to come in with you?' she asked.

I shook my head and she drove off. As I waited in reception, I looked around at the clean white walls, the comfortable chairs, the official notices and signs. It all seemed very alien. I felt like an anthropologist who had just spent a year with some indigenous tribe in a Melanesian island and was finding it hard to readjust to the modern world.

The receptionist called my name, and I walked down the corridor to the room she had indicated.

I knocked on the door and went in. A tall blonde woman stood up to greet me.

'Hi, I'm Dr Williams,' she said. 'And this is Dr Douglas. She's doing her residency here at the moment. Is it OK if she sits in?'

'Yes, of course,' I mumbled, and sat down at the chair opposite the two women, who looked very neat and well dressed. I was wearing muddy old boots, faded blue combat trousers and a baggy woollen sweater. My hair was lank and greasy, and I picked compulsively at the stubble on my chin.

'What brings you here today?'

'I feel like killing myself,' I said.

'When did these feelings start?'

Gradually, I told Dr Williams about the past few months, about the past year, about the Utopia Experiment, about Bo, about everything. Finally, she laid her pen down and asked if she could go and fetch a colleague.

A few minutes later she returned with a smartly dressed Asian man.

'This is Dr Satoshi,' she said. 'He's the senior psychiatrist here.'

Dr Satoshi sat down beside me.

'Dr Williams has told me a bit about your story,' he said. 'I'd like to offer you a bed here for a few days.'

Tears began to well up in my eyes. The thought of staying here, in the hospital, filled me with a sense of relief. But it also scared the hell out of me. But then, surely anything was better than Utopia? I desperately needed to get away from that place, and where else could I go?

'Can I think about it?' I asked.

'Yes, please do,' said Dr Satoshi reassuringly. 'Take your time. Why don't you head down to the cafeteria and get some tea or coffee? You can mull it over there.'

Dr Williams showed me to the cafeteria but I didn't have any money so she bought a cup of tea for me, and left me alone to ponder Dr Satoshi's offer. My head was spinning. What should I do? I kept changing my mind. I would accept the offer. I would politely decline. I would stay in the hospital. I would head straight back to Utopia. I couldn't bear to spend another minute in that hellhole. I couldn't abandon my experiment.

I spent the next few hours like that, sitting in the hospital cafeteria, changing my mind every few seconds. By mid-afternoon I was exhausted.

Dr Williams came into the cafeteria and sat down at my table. I was still gripping the Styrofoam cup, though I had drunk the tea long ago.

'Well?' she said. 'Will you stay?'

'I don't . . . I don't know . . .' I stammered.

'Would you like to see Dr Satoshi again?'

'Yes please.'

So we walked back up the corridor to Dr Satoshi's office, and he once again explained that there was a bed for me here if I wanted it, and that it was his recommendation that I stay here for a few days at least.

'OK,' I said, 'I'll stay.'

Dr Satoshi looked pleased. But just as he reached for a file on his desk, I changed my mind.

'Hold on!' I muttered. 'I don't think I will stay here after all.'

Dr Satoshi looked across at Dr Williams.

She nodded.

Dr Satoshi cleared his throat. 'You're clearly incapable of making decisions,' he said. 'We're going to detain you under the Mental Health Act for your own safety.'

And that was it. I was no longer a free man. From that point on, if I walked out of the hospital on my own, the police would bring me back. And I felt curiously relieved.

14. ESCAPE

During my last week in hospital three of the volunteers came to visit. I was in my room when a nurse told me I had visitors, and I found Agric, Tommy and Pete waiting for me in the common room area in my ward, looking very out of place in their muddy boots and faded jeans.

'How are you doing?' asked Agric, a friendly smile on his face.

'I'm feeling a lot better, thanks. I think I'll be out of this place soon.'

'Well you certainly sound better,' said Agric. 'You've got your voice back at least.'

'It'll do you a world of good to get back into the swing of things,' said Pete. 'Get some fresh air again, do some digging, bake some bread.'

And then it dawned on me; they expected me to just carry on like before, as if nothing had happened! Perhaps they didn't want to believe my mental illness was real, because that would call into question the whole experiment. If the whole thing was merely the product of a deluded mind, what did that say about them? They believed in it all far too much now to let any doubts creep in.

Only when I finally left the experiment would they accept that I had taken leave of my senses. But that would be because I left, not because I started the experiment in the first place. That way they could continue telling themselves that Utopia was a great idea, not a crazy thing dreamt up by a madman. Indeed, you'd have to be mad to leave the place, they thought, because it was something special, an oasis of sanity in a world gone crazy, a refuge from a civilization that was about to implode, a place to create a future from the ashes of the past.

A few days later, Dr Satoshi agreed that I was ready to leave the hospital. I wasn't back to my normal self; far from it. It took me over a year before I felt completely normal again, and even longer before I could be really honest with myself about what had happened in Utopia. But after a month in hospital I was just about functional, and that was a big improvement compared to when I'd arrived.

I shook Dr Satoshi's hand and thanked him for everything he had done for me – for being so frank with me, for taking the time to read some of my writing and telling me that I would write again some day, for not jumping to the wrong diagnosis and giving me anti-psychotic medication. He smiled a broad smile.

'You've had a very narrow escape, Dylan. I don't

think you realize how close you came to a very nasty ending.'

It sounded rather exaggerated, but perhaps he was right.

'May I give you a few last pieces of advice?' he asked.

'Yes, of course.'

'Go somewhere and settle down for a while. Build up a new life for yourself. Give it time. Don't go rushing off again after a year. Put down some roots.'

It didn't sound very appealing, to be honest, but I could see I needed some stability in my life after everything that had happened.

'And one more thing,' he added. 'Don't get involved in a relationship for a while.'

'How long should I wait?' I asked.

'I think three years should be enough.'

Three years! That sounded a bit extreme. But then, I thought, with the first bit of humour in a long time, all I would need to do to follow his advice would be to relay it to any woman who might be interested in me. 'I'm sorry, I can't date you; my psychiatrist says I'm not allowed to go out with anyone for three years.' That would scare them off.

Then I gathered together my belongings – a few clothes and some books – and stuffed them in a big plastic bin liner. And I walked out of the hospital door for the last time.

*

Romay was there to pick me up and take me back to Utopia. I still recall the icy feeling of fear that crept up my spine as I walked down the dirt track and saw the Barn again for the first time in over four weeks. It was a grey, overcast day, and there was nobody in sight.

I pushed open the stiff wooden door and peered inside. Nothing had changed. The same dank smell of fetid water, the unwashed dishes piled up by the make-shift sink, the assortment of tools and breadcrumbs scattered across the big wooden table, the motley collection of old chairs.

I sat down and tried to gather my thoughts. This would be difficult. I had decided to tell the volunteers that the experiment was over, and it was time for everyone to go home. Delivering such a message would be hard at the best of times, but I was still far from well. The anxiety that had overwhelmed me in the weeks leading up to my admission to hospital had diminished somewhat, but it was nonetheless quite debilitating.

Agric appeared at the doorway. His face broke into a warm grin, and he came towards me with his arms outstretched. I let him hug me, and put my arms gingerly around him to hug him back, but I felt like Judas. I couldn't look him in the eye.

'It's over,' I said.

'You mean you're better?'

'No, I mean the experiment is over. I don't believe in it any more.'

'Of course you feel like that now,' said Agric, taking

a seat. 'You've only just come out of hospital. You still need time to recuperate.'

'No,' I said. 'I've made my mind up. It's time for everyone to go home.'

'You can't send people back now, Dylan. It's too late. People believe in this project. They have spent weeks – months in some cases – trying to make this work. You can't end it now.'

I just shook my head. 'I'm sorry,' I said.

Agric suddenly looked ashen-faced. He turned round and went out, leaving me alone in the gloom.

The volunteers, it soon became clear, had no intention of leaving. And there was nothing I could do about that. When Zimbardo ended the Stanford Prison Experiment, he could simply shoo the participants out of the basement of the psychology building. But when you have a bunch of volunteers camped out in the Scottish Highlands, it's not quite so easy to get them to clear off. I soon realized that there was no way I could make them leave if they didn't want to.

To the volunteers, my announcement that the experiment was over was just another symptom of my mental illness, another sign that I hadn't fully recovered. They felt pity for me, they looked after me, they cooked for me and let me rest, but they didn't take me seriously. I was as isolated as ever.

I hadn't anticipated this at all. From the comfort of

my hospital bed, I had imagined everything being much simpler. I would announce that the experiment was over, and everyone would pack up and leave. There would be some cries of protest of course, some recriminations, some tears – but then people would accept the inevitable and start gathering up their belongings. The idea that they would just ignore me and carry on hadn't even crossed my mind.

Now I was flummoxed. It seemed like I was back where I had been before my admission to hospital, watching my experiment rush forward without me, like a horse that had thrown off its rider and was now racing out across the plains, towards who knew what dangers. And then it dawned on me that it wasn't really my experiment any longer, that it hadn't really been my experiment for a while now, that it had evolved into something quite different, and that was actually my way out, because I couldn't leave my own experiment but I could leave if it was someone else's.

And so, quietly and secretly, while the volunteers went about their work, I hatched my escape plan.

Those last few weeks I spent in Utopia, in between being discharged from hospital and making my dramatic escape, felt dreamy and unreal. Outwardly, I guess I didn't seem all that different to the shuffling, shadowy figure who had lumbered around in the weeks preceding my admission to hospital. But inside I felt calmer, and more determined to act. I knew now that at some point soon I would be leaving, and it was just a question of making the necessary arrangements. That was still hard – my ability to plan anything was still severely compromised, and my thoughts were as hazy as ever – but at least I could see a light at the end of the tunnel.

The only times when my anxiety returned were in the evenings; while Agric stoked the Rayburn, and Graham chopped vegetables, I sat in the corner, shaking silently, feeling my body shrink and twist.

I wondered what the other volunteers made of the fact that the founder of the experiment was a mere ghost who hardly said a word, and who looked on, impotent, while his brainchild went on its merry way with scarcely a nod in his direction.

New volunteers continued to arrive. One was Greg Collins, a postal worker from Lancashire. Greg was large and stocky, with a bald head and a large round face. He was in his late thirties, and spoke very slowly. He seemed in a bit of a daze for the first few days, and confided that Utopia was a bit of a culture shock for him, after living in Preston for over twenty years. He also confessed that he had a weak spot for ready-meals, and found it hard to adjust to the idea that you had to plan ahead several hours before eating. But within a week he was happily lighting the Rayburn in the morning and baking bread with Agric, before spending several hours outside gardening or chopping wood. I envied him, and felt sure he must have been disappointed with me for being so useless.

Agric was now fully in charge, though he would often deny it. He was clearly in his element as he scampered about from one task to the next, instructing Pete here in the art of brewing beer, sending Greg out to gather some firewood there, all the while chatting excitedly about the looming financial crisis, which was already gathering like a storm on the horizon.

On 9 August, Agric was jubilant.

'People really wet their pants today!' he announced triumphantly. 'It's beginning, I tell you! In retrospect the global recession may well be seen to have started today.'

He got that right. The active phase of the 2007–8 financial crisis can be dated from precisely that day, after BNP Paribas terminated withdrawals from three hedge funds citing 'a complete evaporation of liquidity'.

Agric had been following all the news with great interest on his little wind-up radio. He told us over supper how the central banks had been forced to step in to provide liquidity so that normal market operations could continue. 'It's happened before,' he remarked, solemnly, 'like just after 9/11, which nailed us to this path we're on now.

'It's an ever higher and stretching thinner tightrope,' he continued, mixing his metaphors. 'It's going to snap sooner or later, you know.'

He forecast a global depression worse than in the

1930s. Combined with the effects of peak oil, it would cause the global financial system to collapse 'within perhaps just a few months', or 'a handful of years' at most. Money would then cease to have any value.

'We've passed the point of no return,' he concluded gravely. 'Our only hope now is to create lifeboat communities like this one, repositories of knowledge and survival skills, and prepare for life after the crash.'

Early one morning in September, while it was still dark and misty, I made my way to the shipping container that held my few remaining possessions. The doors creaked loudly but it was far enough away from the yurts not to wake anyone. I hunted around inside with my torch and retrieved the boxes with my books – unopened for over a year – piling them up one by one on the dirt track nearby. And then I waited for the van to arrive.

With my diminished mental capacities, even something as simple as finding a man with a van to drive my stuff back down to England had been challenging. Sitting there by my boxes of books as the first rays of dawn crept over the hillside, I wasn't even sure whether he would turn up.

When I heard the faint sounds of an engine and then saw the van make its bumpy way down the track towards me, I was still bleary-eyed and not quite sure if it was real. But as we loaded the boxes into the van, I felt a weight slip from my shoulders, and I smiled a genuine smile for the first time in many months. I was free.

After the van had left, I went back to the Barn and found Socrates sleeping by the Rayburn. I picked him up and put him in his cat-box – the same one in which he had made the long journey to Scotland over a year before – but spared him the Valium. I put him on the back seat of my old clapped-out Peugeot 206. It was battered and muddy but it still worked, and I could just about drive. And so, without any farewells, I drove down that old dirt track for the last time, and headed south.

The Utopia Experiment was over. But the volunteers were still there. Later, I learned that they had renamed it the Phoenix Experiment, reflecting their view that it had risen from the ashes of Utopia.

Six years after I left Utopia, Agric was still living on site, for six months each year at least, as if he had 'planted himself there with his tatties,' said Romay. He had converted a part of the Barn into a bedroom, which Angus said was still a dreadful mess. By contrast, his vegetable patch was looking very neat, and had expanded to include a community-funded polytunnel – a makeshift greenhouse made of polyethylene, stretched over a series of hoops.

Several other volunteers would also make occasional visits to the site to help tend the crops and chew the fat with Agric. In December 2009 Greg sent me a Christmas card. He had tracked me down to the university in Ireland where I was teaching, and written a touching message inside the card about how the Utopia Experiment was the best thing that had ever happened to him, and how it gave meaning to his life. Seeing that he worked as a postman and lived alone in a small council flat, it perhaps wasn't so surprising that spending a few weeks now and again in the Scottish Highlands, working outdoors with breathtaking mountains as a backdrop, seemed so wonderful in comparison. But it moved me all the same, and I was glad that, for at least some people if not for me, there had been something utopian about the whole experiment after all.

In 2010 a rumour reached me that the volunteers still expected me to return to Utopia one day, when I had recovered my senses, just in time for the final collapse of civilization, to lead them once again as we all journeyed into the post-apocalyptic future together. It sounded fanciful, as if I had inadvertently created some kind of cult. I'm sure the volunteers never really believed any such thing. In any case, I clearly wasn't cut out to be cult leader.

The first requirement for any cult leader is that he believe his own bullshit. It's amazing how convincing someone can be if they have unshakeable faith, even if what they believe is completely ridiculous. When the poor victims of Jim Jones followed him out to his remote compound in Guyana, his complete and utter certainty must have played a large part in convincing them. And their conviction must surely, in turn, have helped to fuel Jones's certainty, in a mutually reinforcing shared delusion. In my case, however, the more the volunteers believed in me, the less I believed in myself. I'm quite relieved, though, that I didn't have what it takes to be a cult leader. In the end, it was a lack of conviction that saved me.

Adam continued to surprise me. A few days after I arrived back in England, exhausted, to spend some time recuperating at a friend's house in Kent, he emailed me from Germany. He told me he had spent the past few months in Bosnia, living with a farmer who used no machinery.

I shook my head in disbelief. Bosnia? And what the hell was he doing in Germany? How on earth did he manage to do all that travelling with no money?

In November he emailed me again. He was still in Germany, and was building another yurt village. By the following March he was in Austria, and asked me to send him 170 euro so he could buy a new guitar. A few months later I received an email from him in his new guise as 'Father Abraham' in which he invited me to visit the new Rainbow Church website and sign up for an online master class in 'How to Become a Saint in One Mayan Cycle'.

Then I lost touch with Adam completely for several

years. It was not until June 2014, as I was putting the finishing touches to this book, that I heard from him again. Under the subject line 'Healing the past', he wrote that he had some useful information to pass on to a few special people around the world. Apparently, the Great Spirit had informed him that I was one of the lucky few.

Over the course of a few more emails I discovered he was still in Germany, and had reinvented himself as an artist. On one of his webpages, there was a photo of him in a black beret, crisp white shirt and braces, looking every inch the bohemian painter.

I laughed out loud, relieved that the old bugger wasn't dead, as I had feared, and impressed once again at his sheer chutzpah.

15. CIVILIZATION AND ITS DISCONTENTS

It took every last drop of energy and concentration to drive all the way down from the Highlands to the place in Kent where a friend had kindly agreed to let me stay and recuperate from my Scottish odyssey. I spent most of the next two months in bed, getting up only to smoke the occasional cigarette, or drive to the shop to buy frozen pizza, which I would consume, without relish, before diving straight back under the duvet. As I lay in bed, for hours on end, trying to sleep even when I was no longer tired, a memory of Utopia would occasionally flash into my mind, and I would be gripped by a blind panic, an icy terror, and I would shut my eyes even tighter and try to wish myself back into my old cottage in the Cotswolds, as if by sheer force of will I could turn back the clock and erase the whole of the previous year.

I think for a while I seriously believed I might be able to perform that miraculous feat, and it was only slowly that I realized the futility of such magical thinking. As time wore on, I gradually came to accept that I would never be able to go back in time, nor lie in bed for ever; I would have to start rebuilding my life. 'You'll have to start again,' Dr Satoshi had told me, and though it seemed an overwhelming task, an impossibly daunting journey, I finally began to take the first baby steps on what I knew would be a long road ahead. I would spend the morning trying to summon up the courage to face reality, and by midday I would finally crawl out of bed and switch on my computer, and search the web for jobs.

I had burnt all my bridges in Britain, I thought, so I started applying for academic positions abroad. I approached the task with a grim determination, and painfully hacked together a CV, which I emailed joylessly to various universities in Germany, Holland and Ireland. Finally I got invited to a job interview in Cork, on the south coast of the Irish Republic.

The whole process of booking flights, preparing a presentation, and hauling myself over to Ireland was a huge effort, requiring all the concentration and strength I could muster. But a couple of weeks later, there I was, giving a talk on emotions and robots to the assembled professors and post-docs at the Cork Constraint Computation Centre, a research group attached to the Computer Science Department at University College Cork. After a year or so in the wilderness, trying to live without modern technology, I was back in the world of artificial intelligence, knocking on the door of the future that I had once repudiated with such animosity and disdain.

That evening, three of the senior researchers took me

out for dinner in a local Indian restaurant. As we sat round the table ordering curry, my would-be colleagues looked at me eagerly and quizzed me on my recent experience.

'So, what were you doing in Scotland?' asked Nic.

I wondered how to give an honest explanation without making myself seem completely insane.

'Well, it was kind of an experiment in self-sufficiency,' I ventured.

Richard raised his eyebrows and grinned. 'You mean you grew vegetables and stuff?'

'Yes,' I nodded, and took a big gulp of wine to hide my embarrassment.

The others chuckled, and I attempted a smile.

'I just felt I needed a break from academia,' I said. 'I wanted to do something different for a while.'

'And?' said Nic, looking at me quizzically.

'It's a long story,' I said, and drew a deep breath.

And then, just in the nick of time, the waiter arrived with a big plate of poppadoms and a selection of chutneys. By the time we had served ourselves and I had taken my first bite, Richard had, thankfully, changed topic.

By the end of January 2008 I had moved to Ireland and started work at the Cork Constraint Computation Centre, mercifully abbreviated to 4C by its members. I felt awkward going back to work again, and for the first few weeks I would arrive in the lab each morning with a shell-shocked look on my face, only to sit at my desk stabbing aimlessly at the keyboard, trying in vain to give the impression that I knew what I was doing. At lunch-time I would tag along with my colleagues to some local eatery, where I would try to join in the conversation as best I could, all the while feeling disconnected and dazed, like I was just waking up from a heavy slumber.

That feeling dissipated slowly over the following months, until by September or October it was completely gone, and the world felt real again. In the meantime, I started writing about the Utopia Experiment, trying to pull the various notes I had made into some kind of vaguely coherent narrative. But it was hard. Every time I tried to recall the passage of events, I would wince at the painful memories, and I only managed about ten thousand words before I finally gave up and put the whole thing on ice.

Over the following years, my friends would occasion-ally ask me if I had written the book yet. And I would tell them that I had put it on the back burner for now, and would return to it in due course. But as time went on, I became less and less convinced I would ever finish it, and the whole project faded away ever more in-distinctly into the background of my new life.

In 2008 a friend of mine at Futurelab, a non-profit based in Bristol that focused on innovative approaches to teaching and learning, asked me to write a short piece about the experiment for their blog. But I was still unable to look the memories squarely in the face, and unwilling to admit how badly wrong it had all gone. I tried to put a positive spin on everything, and laid the blame for having to end the experiment prematurely on the volunteers. Unfortunately, one of them spotted the piece when it went live, and posted a comment accusing me of falsifying some of the details.

I guessed who it was. It was James Durston, the journalist who had written the article about Utopia for the *Independent* which so upset me when I first read it. It was over a year later, but my wounded pride was still smarting, and I lashed out at him online, accusing him of 'repeating the same nonsense now that you stated in your silly article'.

James came right back at me. 'Silly article?' he replied. 'Read it again, Dylan. Ninety per cent of it is about how much I learnt and enjoyed being there. The few lines I spent on you tucked away near the end are just a description of what I saw in front of me, and what others described. A friend of mine, who also stayed at TUE [the Utopia Experiment] for a few days, met Angus shortly after it was published, and he said it was the only positive article he had seen about the project so far. Don't be so self-absorbed.'

He was right. My own sense of failure still dominated everything I could remember about Utopia, and prevented me from seeing the good side or wondering about how the volunteers had felt about it all. But I was too proud to admit that to James, and I tried to dodge the bullet by accusing him of 'yearning for a strong leader to take control'.

James dismissed my psychobabble with the contempt it deserved. But he agreed that the absence of leadership was an issue. 'The lack of any singular organizing figure-head played the biggest role' in explaining why things didn't work out the way I wanted them to, he observed. 'Without an experimental coordinator, to ensure the volunteers had to innovate to get their necessities,' he argued, 'nor a leader within the group to push things along, things very quickly grew stale, and the place became more of a budget eco-holiday camp than a survivalist experiment.

'While I was there, you were a ghost,' he went on. 'I know you had some personal issues to deal with, but while that may excuse your behaviour it doesn't negate its effects. And I'm pretty sure your issues didn't appear the day I arrived, and disappear the day I left.'

That hurt. But again, it was true.

The volunteers, he told me, 'felt let down when the founder would only appear apparition-like, fleetingly and uselessly, before disappearing again without notice. Your presence actually demoralized people. You say you were a participant-observer; you were neither. You say you were marginalized; I saw none of that. We wanted you to be an active, engaged and productive member of the group, but you appeared incapable.'

Finally, though, James was gracious enough to thank me. 'I don't want to sound too critical,' he said. 'TUE was an experience I will never forget, and many volunteers (myself included) are very grateful to you for having sacrificed so much to set it all up. But it is still frustrating that such a good idea didn't really come close to reaching its potential, for the simple lack of a bit of project management.'

I knew he was right, but I still couldn't admit it in public. And the same unwillingness to tell it like it was kept me from returning to the manuscript I had started, and which lay unfinished while I busied myself with rebuilding my academic career. It would take me almost six years before I was finally ready to write this book and admit, in public, that the blame for what went wrong lay not with the volunteers, but with me.

One day in April 2013 I called my mother on the phone.

'I've decided to finish the Utopia book,' I told her.

She let out a small gasp of surprise. 'I thought you'd given up on that project,' she said.

'I kind of had. But it was always there in the background.'

'Well.' She paused. 'I bet it will be rather different from the book you thought you'd write when you started the experiment!'

That, I thought to myself, was an understatement.

When our ancestors gave up their nomadic existence and started farming, some ten or eleven thousand years ago, they drove the first nail into the coffin of self-sufficiency. Farming is more efficient than hunting and gathering, so some people could stop producing food and devote their time to other things like making clothes and building houses. They were now dependent on others to provide food for them. But it wasn't until the Industrial Revolution that this process reached escape velocity.

At the end of the eighteenth century, farmers still made up 90 per cent of the labour force in the US; two centuries later, it is only 2 per cent. There has been a corresponding explosion in the diversity and specialization of the non-food-producing occupations. When Plato wrote about the division of labour, he argued that 'the minimum state would consist of four or five men' – a farmer, a builder, a weaver, and one or two others. The 2010 Standard Occupational Classification system used by federal statistical agencies in the US lists 840 different occupations.

With all this diversity comes growing interdependence. Even something as apparently simple as a pencil is the product of hundreds of different people. In Leonard Reed's little essay 'I, Pencil', the pencil itself declares:

> Now, you may say that I go too far in relating the picker of a coffee berry in far off Brazil and food growers elsewhere to my creation; that this is an extreme position. I shall stand by my claim. There isn't a single person in all these millions, including

the president of the pencil company, who contributes more than a tiny, infinitesimal bit of know-how. From the standpoint of know-how the only difference between the miner of graphite in Ceylon and the logger in Oregon is in the type of know-how. Neither the miner nor the logger can be dispensed with, any more than can the chemist at the factory or the worker in the oil field – paraffin being a by-product of petroleum.

The pencil argues that this merits our 'wonder and awe', but the tangled web of global interconnections can also be anxiety provoking. It can lead to a sense of helplessness, as the Unabomber argued. Some react, as he did, and Thoreau before him, by setting off on a deluded quest to regain that self-sufficiency our ancestors lost, ignoring the fact that even hunter-gatherers live in groups. The idea that modern civilization might soon collapse only makes our interdependence more worrying. The anxiety that doomers feel when contemplating the modern world is ultimately rooted in a solipsistic hankering for a Robin Crusoe existence.

But the Unabomber was wrong, and the pencil was right. It is good that no man is an island. These global ties bind us together. Even such apparently simple products as pencils are the result of thousands of strangers cooperating.

According to the economist Paul Seabright, 'citizens of the industrialized market economies have lost their

sense of wonder at the fact that they can decide spontaneously to go out in search of food, clothing, furniture
and thousands of other useful, attractive, frivolous or
life-saving items and when they do so, somebody will
have anticipated their actions and thoughtfully made
such items available for them to buy'.

Paradoxically, Seabright argues, such cooperation is
only made possible by a kind of tunnel vision. By this he
means 'the capacity to play one's part in the great complex enterprise of creating the prosperity of a modern
society without knowing or necessarily caring very much
about the overall outcome'. If we all went around
wondering about how the global economy worked, or
even how to make a pencil by ourselves, the whole
system would grind to a halt. We would all be overwhelmed by analysis paralysis.

If self-sufficiency is an illusion, then so is sustain-
ability. Nothing is truly sustainable, in the sense of
potentially lasting for ever. Everything runs out in the
end. It's just a question of time.

Environmentalists say that deep-sea trawling is not
sustainable because it depletes fish stocks faster than they
can renew themselves. Radical ecologists say that modern
civilization is not sustainable because it relies on oil,
which is a finite resource. A sustainable civilization
would presumably run entirely on renewable resources.
But nothing is truly renewable, and all the fish will
eventually be gone, and the wind will blow no more, for
a billion years from now, the oceans will boil away as the

sun grows into a supernova. The only way humans will survive then is by leaving the earth and colonizing other planets. But an interplanetary lifestyle won't be sustainable either, because eventually the stars will burn themselves out and become black holes and the entire universe will become a cold, quiet place, where nothing ever happens.

Given that everything will come to an end eventually, does it really matter if humanity lasts another million years rather than just another thousand? Since civilization is bound to collapse sooner or later, does it matter when?

And why should we worry about the human race anyway? Does it matter what happens to the rest of humanity after we die? If we have children, we care what happens to them, of course, and presumably about their children too, but how many generations more can we really care about? And if our descendants fail to leave any children at some point, as must happen to them all eventually when the human race perishes, why should we care about the species as a whole? Is such concern really just a fig leaf for our worries about our own mortality, a secular substitute for the eternal life we long for even when we know we can't have it?

Nick Bostrom thinks that the inevitable end of the human race need not invalidate our hopes for the future of humanity, because what counts is not eternal survival, but the realization of our full potential as a species, whatever that may be. But then surely we can say the same thing about the individual human life? What counts is not eternal life, which for atheists like me is a pipe dream anyway, but realizing one's full potential – becoming the best person that one can possibly be. And if we do that, we can die in peace, whether we survive the apocalypse or not, and regardless of what happens to those who come after us.

Pinker is right to say that Hobbes was a better anthropologist than Rousseau, but that does not mean he was a better philosopher. Hobbes was right in thinking that our hunter-gatherer ancestors led lives that were nasty, brutish and short, but he thought there was a way to remedy this. By submitting to a strong sovereign, we can at least live in relative peace. It won't be a Utopia, but it will be better than the continual war of all against all.

This is a limited form of optimism, but optimism it still is. Rousseau, on the other hand, saw only slavery in the modern state. Even today, I feel this is closer to the truth. And we get still closer by combining the insights of both philosophers. To Hobbes, we owe the realization that there was no Golden Age, no garden of Eden. From Rousseau we learn that progress has been a double-edged sword. Yes, technologies have improved, and the powers of science have increased. We live longer, healthier lives than our ancestors ever did, and we should be grateful for these small mercies. But these changes have not resulted in any fundamental amelioration of the human condition. Every step forward is, from another equally valid perspective, a step closer to the end of the world. Progress inevitably metamorphoses into its opposite. In the long run we are all dead. Even if humans discover how to prolong their lives indefinitely, the universe will eventually unravel and freeze. And then there will be nothingness for ever and ever, and permanent darkness.

But this need not lead to despair. If we confront this basic fact, if we look it straight in the face, unflinchingly, we may go temporarily insane. But we may emerge from the other side of this dark night of the soul with some tranquility, some greater equanimity, and enjoy what little is left to us of this short, hard, beautiful life.

It was 2012, the year the Maya thought the world would come to an end. Actually, they didn't really think that at all; 21 December 2012 simply marked the end of one *baktun* – a time period in the Mayan Long Count calendar – and the beginning of the next. But such historical niceties didn't bother the New Age prophets and opportunistic journalists who pumped out increasingly fanciful speculations as the date approached. One month before the dreaded cataclysm, I was back in the land of the Maya, where the idea for the Utopia Experiment had first come to me, seven years previously.

It was Thanksgiving, and some of my students had decided to cook a traditional American Thanksgiving dinner. I was spending a semester at UFM, a university in Guatemala City, and it felt rather incongruous to be eating turkey and cranberry sauce in the hot midday sun. After the meal, the students passed around some cardboard cut-out hands. They had traced around their open palms on thin coloured card and cut round the outline to make a set of red, yellow and orange hand-shaped pieces. We were supposed to take one each and write on it one thing we felt particularly thankful for. Then we would stick them all on a cardboard tree, which was decorated with a red notice at the bottom on which the words 'I'm thankful for . . .' were inscribed in big black letters.

I didn't have to ponder my answer for very long. It was something I thought about every day, and especially whenever I felt sad or disappointed. It always worked; as soon as I thought about it, my mood would lift. It was a good trick, and as a result I had rarely been miserable for very long ever since I had left Utopia. Or perhaps that was simply due to the fact that I had been on a low dose of antidepressants all that time too.

I stuck my cardboard hand on the Thanksgiving tree. It read:

'I'm not living in a field in Scotland.'

And, you know what? I'm glad I did it. Not just because I learned to value things that I previously scorned, like the flawed social institutions that have evolved in their higgledy-piggledy way over hundreds of years, or the myriad little technological developments that make our lives more comfortable than those of our ancestors, from toilet paper to toothpaste. And not just because I'm not living in a field in Scotland any more, either.

I'm glad because I learned something even more valuable. I learned that I'm not invincible, but also that I'm stronger than I thought. And I'm not afraid any more.

I'm not afraid of losing everything I have, and ending up in hospital again, or even living in a field again, if that's where my winding path takes me. And I'm not afraid of the collapse of civilization either – not because I no longer think it will collapse – who knows? – but because now I've looked that possibility squarely in the face.

In his 1757 treatise on aesthetics, *A Philosophical Enquiry into the Origin of Our Ideas of the Sublime and Beautiful*, Edmund Burke notes that fear is heightened by obscurity. The monster is always more terrifying when his face is hidden. Conversely, 'when we know the full extent of any danger, when we can accustom our eyes to it, a great deal of the apprehension vanishes.' I spent a year trying to get as clear a picture as possible of the collapse of civilization. It almost killed me, but it also purified me, as if it drained every last drop of fear in my body. I stared into the abyss, and I almost fell in, but somehow I came back from the brink and lived to tell the tale.

In her book, *The Top Five Regrets of the Dying*, Bronnie Ware writes of the clarity of vision that people gain at the end of their lives, and how we might learn from their wisdom. 'When questioned about any regrets they had or anything they would do differently,' she says, 'common themes surfaced again and again.'

What people regretted most of all was that they hadn't followed their dreams. Again and again the patients she was nursing would ask her: 'Why didn't I just do what I wanted?'

Most people had not honoured even half of their dreams, and had to die knowing that this was due to choices they had made, or not made. And the thing that stopped them was fear. They felt the weight of social expectation, and lacked the courage to throw off the shackles of convention.

Whatever happens now, I know I won't have that regret. My dream may have turned into a nightmare, but at least I followed it. I won't sit around in my old age, wondering what would have happened if I had put that crazy plan into action, instead of carrying on with my job as a university lecturer.

And I'm not afraid of doing something equally crazy again, if the thought so takes me.

Glossary

boomer Someone who thinks that technological progress will continue indefinitely and will make us all richer and happier.

catastrophism The belief that the world is heading towards an economic, environmental, social or spiritual collapse, and that a new and better world will emerge from the ashes of the old one.

cornucopian See *boomer*.

declinism The belief that things are getting worse, compared to some former Golden Age. Popular candidates for the moment when the decline started include the Industrial Revolution (romanticism) and the birth of agriculture (primitivism).

doomer Someone who believes that a global catastrophe is imminent, and that civilization will collapse as a result.

millennialism The belief that the imperfect world we live in will soon be destroyed and replaced with a better one.

prepper   Someone who is actively preparing for a disaster by stocking up on food and other items so they can survive. The disaster could be anything from an extended power cut to a global catastrophe. Thus not all preppers are doomers; some preppers do not think a global catastrophe is imminent, and are only preparing for a relatively small disaster.

primitivism   The belief that modern civilization makes people unhappy and that the cure lies in returning to a more simple way of living in natural surroundings.

rewilding   The process of reversing human domestication by relearning primitive skills such as hunting and gathering.

survivalist   Someone who is actively preparing for a disaster by stocking up on food and other items so they can survive. Unlike preppers, survivalists tend to think the disaster will be a global or at least a national catastrophe. Thus most survivalists are doomers.

transhumanist   Someone who hopes that future developments in technology will radically transform human nature for the better.

picador.com

blog
videos
interviews
extracts